CEO.OLOGY

Outthink the
Limits of What's Possible

MALCOLM ALLEN

CEO.OLOGY

Copyright © 2019 by **Malcolm Allen**

Web: www.Unconditional.org
ISBN: 9781072379997

CONTENTS

INTRODUCTION

C EO—that's the business term for the one in charge, the Chief Executive Officer. This is the person who makes the decisions, sees that they are carried out, and takes responsibility—whether it be blame or praise—for results.

Our president is a CEO, as is every governor or mayor. One of our most quotable presidents, Harry Truman, made two famous statements that tell a lot about what goes into being a CEO. One he had made into a sign that he put on his desk in the Oval Office: "The buck stops here." The other came in a time of crisis, when he responded to a questioner by saying: "If you can't stand the heat, get out of the kitchen." Those quotes go to the heart of a CEO's responsibilities.

Truman's point was that, as the nation's CEO, he had to be ready, willing, and able to deal with every situation the government faced. The same is true of legendary CEOs like Robert Johnson of Black Entertainment Television, the late Steve Jobs of Apple, or even the owner of a corner grocery store (who is also its CEO). The achievements of leaders like Truman, Jobs, and Johnson came from a combination of their vision, their collaboration with others, and their willingness to take responsibility for their actions. They had the courage to face their failures, and they always shared the credit for success.

CEO.OLOGY is my term for the art of being a decision-maker. It covers principles that are absolutely essential to someone starting a business, or to a manager of an existing business. It can apply to the person who directs a smaller section of a larger enterprise, whether public or private. CEO.OLOGY will prove useful to anyone who has the responsibility of directing the efforts of others. But, at its core, it is a way of training yourself to do what it takes to succeed. If you master the basics of CEO.OLOGY you can make a fortune, change the world, or even do both.

Whether you are organizing a huge new entrepreneurial challenge involving many coworkers and consumers, or simply applying for your first job, you should understand, and master, the skills of CEO.OLOGY. If you're going to be the boss, you will need to begin cultivating these skills immediately. If you are a boss of others, but you too also have a boss you must answer to (usually in a large business, such as a major corporation), you need to know how to deal with your responsibilities, while understanding how these fit into your employer's overall plan. If you're applying for a job—even that first part-time job when you're still in high school—CEO.OLOGY will help you understand how the business world works. It will give you the tools to manage yourself and collaborate with others. It will help you unlock your potential for greatness so that you can fully experience a wide world of possibilities. In short, no matter who you are, or what work you do, it will help you succeed!

What are these principles? They are simple guidelines that will help you solve the most complex problems. Among them are the CEO's three Rs: Reinvent, Rethink, and Rewire.

What does it mean to "Reinvent"? Whether you're starting a new business, or applying for an entry-level job, you want to look at your skills and potentials, then at your goals, and reshape your emotions and attitudes to fit this new world you're entering. This doesn't mean you have to try to be something you're not. It means you want to tap into who you really are, and find the motivations and energy to be all that you can be in this new position. You reinvent your way of thinking about yourself, adjusting your attitude to excel in your new duties.

And how about "Rethink"? That means looking at what you are about to do from new and different perspectives. When you rethink a problem, it's often a productive time for collaboration with others. It's reaching out to coworkers, clients, and customers, seeking their intelligence and insights, so that you can see the various routes that have the potential for success. When you begin something new, your first thought is always about how it will affect you. That's natural, but your personal concerns should only be a starting point. You need to rethink this new effort in terms of the other people it affects. What do you have to do to be a good boss? Or, if you're working for other people, what are their needs? If you're hiring employees, what kind of people will best serve you and your company in achieving stated goals? Or, if you're the one being hired: How can your talents help you achieve the goals of your employer? When you think about everyone else's needs, you can do a better job of understanding your own strengths and weaknesses, and you can put your best foot forward.

The third R is "Rewire." Up until now your focus has been you. You automatically think of your own wants and needs. But you also need to rewire your thought processes so that you automatically reach out to that broader world out there. You must open your mind to the ideas, hopes, and dreams of employees, colleagues, and consumers. Be ready to learn new approaches. Tap into experience—and not just your own—to gain answers to surprising questions. Realize your potential by making yourself accountable for greater and greater responsibilities. Learn to collaborate with others, and to respect and honor their dreams and aspirations, just as you do your own.

Along with these come basic principles that most of us already know, but we often lose track of them. In our day-to-day lives we might not even notice if we aren't acting by these tried-and-true principles. In our personal affairs, most of us occasionally allow our emotions to pull us this way or that, subtly creating unconscious and unintentional decisions that come back to hurt us later. When we only have to consider ourselves, the effects are usually minor, but in the workplace every action we take can affect many other people: those we work with, those our enterprise serves, and the overall community.

Among these principles is that of lifelong learning. A basic requirement of CEO.OLOGY is to see every decision as an opportunity to discover new things. We must courageously welcome fresh ideas and information, even if they go against our previous assumptions. Another fundamental you will master is the practice of treating every error you make as an opportunity to learn how to do it right. This doesn't mean you have to pursue mistakes as you would goals, but it does mean that even our miscues can have value if we're willing to find creative, effective solutions.

We'll look at the role perspective plays in the workplace. Any successful entrepreneur knows that ideas can grow stale, and people can get set in their ways. A method that's effective today might only breed failure in future situations, but our memories of its earlier successes might persuade us to stick with it long after it's stopped working. We should always keep ourselves open to smart innovation and revision. We should even develop the habit of seeking out constructive criticism, even when—particularly when—we are about to begin a new project, or phase of a project.

These principles are just a sample of what you will learn as you read on.

To illustrate these points we will show you how they've worked in the lives of some of the most famous celebrities of our time. From Oprah we'll discover how to avoid falling into the trap of depending on others to do what we should be doing ourselves to fulfill our dreams. From Bill O'Reilly we'll see the value of hearing all sides, and considering alternative methods and solutions, while coming to our own conclusions. And, once we're in the world of celebrities, how can we avoid Kim Kardashian when dealing with the subject of self-love and self-esteem? If you're going to be a boss, you need a lot of confidence, and that's KK's signature quality.

Along with the rich and famous, we will also look at examples and composites from real-life situations among people like ourselves: the construction worker who strikes out on his own to become a unique kind of contractor, the beautician who has a vision of opening her own kind of salon dealing with both inner and outer beauty, and the recently retired man who sees a business opportunity in helping kids everywhere learn the skills they'll need most once they've left the classroom. We'll look at the teenager applying for her first job, and the senior citizen who's tired of vegetating through his golden years and envisions a way to create profitable work for himself and others.

CEO.OLOGY will tell all these stories, and more. When you've finished you will be able to take its principles and compare them to the world you see through your own eyes. As you do this, you can test its arguments against your own experiences and observations. You will find that it works. Once you've taken the principles of CEO.OLOGY to heart, you can use this book as a guide to make them work for you.

CEO.OLOGY begins with you. It can't happen without you. You are like a seed in a packet. You could grow into a mighty tree that will go on to produce strong branches and rich green leaves that give shade while replenishing the earth's atmosphere—or you can sit in that packet. But a seed doesn't do it alone. A seed is only a tiny indicator of potential. It needs water, nutrition, sunlight, and more, and it needs them every day throughout its long life. CEOs and those workers who are potential CEOs need coworkers, clients, customers, and colleagues who will help them and their enterprises grow. Recognizing the links between all these people, and learning how to work with others, is the core of CEO.OLOGY.

Every person must begin by becoming their own boss—their own CEO. From there, the sky is the limit! What follows is a way to do this, and do it well!

REVERSE ENGINEERING
OF THE MIND

We learn many of life's basics through a process of rote; that is, repetition, or mechanical routine. Many children learn their ABCs this way. When we hear a class of preschoolers chirping out the alphabet song, their teachers are using a rote method (in this case, one that's rhythmic and fun) to etch these building blocks of language into their brains. It works. Just about all of us know some version of the alphabet song.

Rote methods are great for ABCs, certain driving skills, and many other basic functions of our lives. In business we often want to create repetitive or rote methods for accounting, inventory, taxes, and other necessities. These are huge issues, but, as any good teacher knows, rote behavior has its limits.

When we start a business, or any other complex venture, rote methods play a role, but they aren't enough. Though habit and memorization might help us gain the disciplines we need to succeed, creativity and flexibility are just as essential. We must reach into ourselves, and encourage others, to find innovative ideas. As a recent cliché goes: we must think outside the box.

Success comes most often to those who can master both rote and innovation in the right proportions. What's the right proportion? That changes, depending on what you're doing. An accountant will rely more on standard rote methods than a stockbroker. The accountant relies on known quantities and precise operations. The rules of the job are clear. On the other hand, the stockbroker is judged by the accuracy of his or her predictions. That requires a combination of imagination, analysis, and common sense.

Rote methods are the cautious, conservative side of any venture. They protect us by giving us a foundation on which to build, and laying down a baseline for measurements of progress. Every successful business needs those. The difference between any two well-conceived business ventures is in the innovations. Those are the things that will excite investors, and inspire coworkers and consumers.

When we begin something new, such as a job search or a new business, we often guard ourselves against threats and avoid pitfalls. We assume that if we make sure nothing goes wrong, everything is going to go right. When we're stuck in this defensive mode of thinking, we concentrate almost entirely on the negatives. Though identifying a problem is an essential step toward solving it, we also need to take positive actions, including those that involve risk. We can't simply avoid pitfalls. We have to constantly aim at making better, more effective efforts.

When our thinking is stuck in negative territory, that's when we need to use "reverse engineering," that is, create a reversed infrastructure in our minds. We have to be like the highway planner who looks at jammed-up traffic patterns, then reroutes various lanes, and even whole highways. Exits become entrances, and vice versa; one-way streets become two-way; some traffic lights are added, and others are eliminated. This frees up the traffic jams, allowing us to see all our options, good and bad. Avoiding bad choices and dangerous situations makes sense, but it shouldn't be the basis of our entire approach. Avoiding all risk might ward off failure, but it also stops our chances for success. We should begin each day by reversing this negative attitude. We do this by altering our normal mental processes. It's like a reverse engineering of our entire thought process. We concentrate on our choices, ranging from conservative to radical, so that we can take positive steps in the right direction.

This is our daily mind calibration. A lot of this calibration involves recognizing and raising our "EQ"—the emotional equivalent of IQ. We want our emotions to spark our enthusiasm, but when our feelings spiral out of control, that can undermine every smart move we've made. If we always consider others—those we're going to work with, and those we seek to serve—that will keep us from falling into this trap. Close collaboration with others is like a reality check. It forces us to look at what we have to offer, and how that fits with the needs of others. One famous entrepreneur who shows a gut understanding of the importance of collaboration is Jay Z.

Jay Z grew up without a father in a Brooklyn housing project, then went on to amass a fortune of over a half billion dollars. His modest beginnings included a checkered youth marked by violence, the drug trade, and other troubles common to life in the 'hood. On his twelfth birthday, his mom gave him a boom box, and this sparked his interest in music. It was the early 1980s, and rappers were just beginning to make their mark on the music scene.

While in his teens, Jay Z began freestyling, composing his own lyrics, and performing for anyone who might be willing to watch and listen. He followed the artists of the up-and-coming rap scene, imitating the ones he liked. He gradually evolved a style of his own. By the early 1990s he was beginning to make a name for himself. In his early career, Jay Z worked as a backup performer on recordings by pioneer rapper Jaz-O. But from the start, Jay Z had been searching for his own niche, and in 1993 he released his first rap single, "In My Lifetime." Lacking a record company, he sold CD copies out of the trunk of his car.

On stage and in the studio, music is most often a collaborative venture. Jay Z was learning to work with others, sometimes adapting to their musical visions, other times inspiring them with his own. It was an education based in cooperation.

Nonetheless, Jay Z had a lot to learn. That rap scene of the '80s and '90s was often a war zone, marked by violent disputes and even some high-profile murders. Jay Z had his own set of feuds, including one that set him and Jaz-O against each other. Compared to several other clashes, Jay Z's skirmishes were minor, but they were still serious enough to give him a secure place in the pantheon of "gangsta" culture. His conflicts with rival rappers could turn violent, and in 1999 resulted in a stabbing incident that brought him three years' probation.

Eventually Jay Z worked his way through most of these troubles and began releasing a steady stream of hits. One platinum record followed another, selling millions worldwide. As he began investing his profits in a wide range of enterprises, Jay Z the rapper transformed into Jay Z the businessman. His ventures included investments in record companies, clothing companies, and a share of the NBA's Brooklyn Nets. He learned the skills of leadership, salesmanship, and cooperation with others. He brought his own individual vision to his work, saying: "My brands are an extension of me."

Jay Z has been rewarded with fame and huge riches, but he's not resting on his laurels. Recently he sold his interest in the Nets so that he could start his own sports management group, Roc Nation Sports, which will represent professional athletes. Is it a risk? Yes. Sports management can be an incredibly lucrative business, but most sports agencies fail, or are bought out within the first two years. Why is Jay Z's effort a better bet than most? First, because he's done his homework, learning about the field as part-owner of a team, and second because he knows how to collaborate with others. Jay Z has grown up from the mercurial gangsta rapper of yesteryear into the incredibly rich and innovative entrepreneur we know today. He has a net worth of a half billion dollars to prove it.

But what about those of us starting on a smaller scale? What can we learn from a celebrity like Jay Z? Let's look at a non- celebrity.

A good place to start would be with seventeen-year-old Troy. Troy has grown up in an atmosphere similar to that of Jay Z's upbringing. Though thirty years have passed, much remains the same. Troy's father left before he was born, and his mom has raised him alone. At thirteen Troy got in trouble for a violent altercation at school. At fourteen he tried working as a runner for a local crack pusher. An understanding minister then took Troy aside, using an approach that mixed stern discipline with gentle understanding. "You can make some money in crime right now, and next week, and maybe the week after that," the minister told him, "but soon odds are that you'll be on the inside of a cell in juvie. There you'll learn how to score big bucks in ways that will keep you going and coming from prison for the rest of your days—unless you run into that bullet that's got your name on it. There's a better way."

The minister got Troy into a summer youth program in an upstate town. The paychecks didn't even amount to minimum wage, but the boys received room and board in a local school dormitory, and the necessary transportation. They worked different temp jobs each week, with each job in a different field. One week Troy swept floors in a small electronics store, but for two hours a day he learned about the newest mobile devices. Another week he unloaded trucks for a supermarket, with instruction about inventory, and how to organize a stockroom. There was even a week when he labored on a nearby dairy farm. A lifelong city kid, Troy was amazed when he found he was pretty good at milking cows and running a henhouse.

Troy's summer didn't start out easy. He was in an unfamiliar place. He'd never worked a real job before, and now he was learning new jobs every week. At first he felt like a fish out of water, but he quickly realized that all the other boys were having as difficult a time as he was. By the second week he felt as if he could survive the summer. In the third week he realized he was learning real skills. By the fourth week he was starting to have fun. Soon Troy realized he could learn any task they threw at him. He lost any fears he'd had.

Troy was a quick study. Over that summer he had to adapt to new bosses and coworkers every week. In small shops he interacted with customers, learning some of the basics of salesmanship and public relations. When the town hall put him with its janitorial crew, he had his first look at public service. It was a baptism of fire in the world of cooperation and collaboration. He was learning how enterprises worked, and how to get along with people. He did so well that he was asked back the following summer. In some ways it was more of the same, but the program directors also made him his dorm's chief resident. This got him better pay to go with his senior status. All the other boys were first-year workers. Troy learned to listen, to empathize, and to help them solve problems.

Now home, and back on his city streets, Troy has no use for the drug peddlers. Luckily he wasn't in too deep. Instead he's finishing high school, and has a part-time job usually given to one of the more enterprising students from nearby colleges: supervising the four young delivery drivers for the evening shift at a large pizzeria. All four of the drivers are older than he is, but Troy looks older than his years, and he exudes the authority of experience. He plans to attend college, and eventually start his own pizza business. He dreams of owning a chain of them, a dream that's slowly becoming a concrete plan.

Though Troy may never amass a fortune as large as Jay Z's (few of us ever do), he's bound to succeed. Like the super-rich rapper, he's learned from his experiences, both good and bad. He realizes that any mistake is an invitation to learn something valuable. He knows better than to encourage bad things to happen, but if they do, he'd ready to take the resulting lessons to heart. His delivery drivers like their jobs, largely due to his positive attitude and organizational skills. In a quiet way he inspires them to work together. Troy's boss wishes Troy would forget about college, and come to work for him full-time. Troy routinely (and diplomatically) refuses this offer. He knows education is one of the keys to his future success.

Troy had started out with two strikes against him. He was poor, and he'd fallen into criminal activities at an early age. But when he finally pulled himself together, he changed course by reversing his thinking. He no longer thought only about himself, and what was in it for him. He looked at the long haul, and allowed himself to be trained to see the needs of others. He'd come from the world of drug peddling, whose customers are hooked on products that will ultimately bring them down. He learned that the best businesses sell services and products that people can enjoy without addiction and self-destruction. On the street he'd learned that having an edge was dependent on weapons and muscle. Profits came from the barrel of a gun. Now he sees ways to make long-term profits for himself and others through smarts, hard work, and intelligent decisions that take everyone into account.

Jay Z had a similar experience as he climbed the ladder in entertainment. He let himself get swept up in feuds and violence, allowing his emotions to rule his intellect. When faced with the possibility of losing his freedom, he began to learn the lessons of responsibility. That put him on the road to becoming a husband, father, and one of the richest entrepreneurs in show business.

You can do the same thing. If you're stuck in the rut of unemployment, or of accepting high-risk jobs in someone's criminal enterprises, you're caught in a negative frame of mind in which you always have to look out for yourself to the exclusion of all others. That's how it works on the wrong side of the law—

every man for himself. To reverse this thinking, you must begin by reversing your situation. Find a legitimate job. Accept lower pay in return for the opportunity to learn new skills. Reach out to empathize with your employer. Listen to your superiors, and find out what they need. Cooperate with your coworkers, and look for the most effective ways to serve your customers.

The immediate profits won't be as great as the pay from illegal enterprises, but you will be laying the foundation for a long life of happy, productive work. And the potential for profits becomes unlimited.

Failure by Design: Never a Mistake, Always a Lesson

When we take risks, we're bound to win some and lose some. In the real world this is inevitable. We should never plan to fail, but if something we do doesn't work, we must always be poised to take advantage of the error by examining it, learning what went wrong, and finding a solution. No matter how disastrous it is, we should never look at a failure in terms of blame. We should welcome the opportunity to improve and perfect our approach.

Steve Jobs

A great example was set by the late Steve Jobs of Apple. When Jobs was still in his early twenties, he and a partner cofounded Apple. It was the 1970s, when few had even heard of Silicon Valley, and "digital" was barely a blip on the public's consciousness. Even then Jobs predicted the coming popularity of personal computers in homes. He marketed the early Apple systems to fill that need. In the early 1980s, Jobs oversaw the development of the first MacIntosh computer, then helped bring about a brilliant promotion campaign to sell it.

Despite these triumphs, Jobs was losing support within his own company. It was a time when the whole industry was on a roller-coaster ride. Companies started, succeeded, then failed, all in just a few months. The stresses were huge, and many wondered how any CEO could stand such pressure. Jobs was not immune. Employees who worked for him at Apple in the mid-1980s described Jobs as erratic, temperamental, and arrogant. He would call a meeting for six in the evening, then keep participants there until long after midnight. A simple walk down a corridor might involve several confrontations. Workers didn't even want to share the same elevator with Jobs. It was said that between the upper floors and the lobby he'd impulsively fire workers for little or no reason. His successes had lured him into thinking he could do no wrong. It wasn't long before he learned how mistaken he was.

By May of 1985 some colleagues feared Jobs was out of control. Many of his friends were worried, and some in the company were fast becoming former friends. Jobs hardly noticed the change. Though he was unaware of it, his partner had plans to force him out. When Jobs began to suspect something was wrong, he called a board meeting, where he planned to turn the tables, and fire his partner. This may have been his most fateful miscalculation. When the board met, the two had a showdown. The board supported his partner. Jobs was out.

Jobs later described his reaction to his firing this way: "The heaviness of being successful was replaced by the lightness of being a beginner again, less sure about everything. It freed me to enter one of the most creative periods of my life . . . none of this would've happened if I hadn't been fired from Apple." That rosy view was far from evident at the time. Leaving the company he'd cofounded was a serious blow, but Jobs began to realize he could learn from this debacle. He wasn't without talent, smarts, and resources. He knew how to start a new company; he'd done that before. Now he would do it again, and this time he wouldn't fall into the same traps. He reviewed actions he'd taken, both right and wrong. He found himself wanting to try it again, but this time he would do better. This time Jobs would keep his feet on the ground.

Within a year he'd founded NeXT Computer. When he needed cash to keep his start-up afloat, he got capital from billionaire Ross Perot, in exchange for part-ownership. Perot knew genius when he saw it, and didn't interfere with his new partner. He just sat back and watched NeXT grow.

In the decade that followed, Jobs built NeXT into a hugely profitable company. He used some of those profits to buy a graphics division that had been developed by George Lucas, maker of the Star Wars movies. Jobs transformed this graphics team into what soon took the name of "Pixar." In this role he acted as an executive producer on the huge hit movie, *Toy Story*, which used Pixar's images. This led to more collaborations between Pixar and Disney.

In 1996 Jobs sold NeXT to the company that had fired him eleven years before. Apple paid $427 million for the company. As a part of the deal he returned to work at Apple in a leadership role. The following year he was back in control of his old company, taking over as Apple's acting CEO when the then-current chief was fired. Over the next decade Apple established itself as one of the most innovative giants in any field. Most dominant companies find a signature product or service, then spend years and even decades tweaking and expanding on that one theme. But Jobs wasn't content with that.

Year after year he hosted public unveilings of new products that excited the imagination. He created his own format and style for these presentations, making his marketing method a part of the brand itself. The iPod had revolutionized the way music is delivered, and the way people listen to it. Few products have brought bigger, more rapid changes to a major industry. Vast music libraries would now fit in your pocket. The iPad popularized the tablet, and garnered most of that market until imitative competitors sprang up. The iPhone set all the major precedents for what a smartphone was and could be. Jobs timed each product introduction for maximum impact, and soon his presentations were receiving more news coverage than most presidential news conferences. Competitors were left far behind.

What had changed? Jobs had. He'd learned from his failure. He now realized that his arrogance, perfectionism, and 24/7 work ethic wasn't getting him where he wanted to go. He became more adaptable, and he learned to recognize the need for change and revision. As one colleague has said of him: "More so than any person I ever met in my life, [Jobs] had the ability to change his mind . . . Maybe the most underappreciated thing about Steve was that he had the courage to change his mind."

It took courage. Jobs had been the poster child for workaholics and control freaks. With little conscious intent, he'd allowed himself to become the kind of CEO whom others feared. Jobs still believed in hard work, and making each product as close to perfect as possible, but now he understood the need to lighten up a little. He saw that this effort helped to get the creativity flowing in his own mind, and in the minds of his people. With Jobs' new attitude ruling company decisions, Apple produced one of the most astonishing outpourings of innovation in the history of business and technology. In less than a decade, Jobs not only turned Apple around, he also spearheaded its race past Microsoft as the world's leader in digital consumer products.

In 1985, on the eve of his fateful firing from Apple, Jobs was the same phenomenal combination of intellect and ambition that he'd always been, and always would be. That was his basic personality. But he'd used his talents to propel others forward at an ever-increasing pace, discarding anyone who couldn't keep up. He allowed no room for give-and-take, and only listened to ideas that complemented his own thoughts. Apple was a young company in a young field, and that demanded an open approach informed by a consistent philosophy. Instead the company had suffered under the limitations of Jobs' increasing instability. Lost in the currents of his own personal creativity, he lost his capacity to recognize the best ideas of others. He wasn't growing, and as long as he was at the helm, Apple wouldn't grow either.

Once he was on his own, Jobs learned quickly. He took a long look at himself, and realized he'd been wrong. He admitted this to himself, and confessed it to the world. In years to come he said so in books, interviews, and speeches. It was like watching a speaker at an AA meeting. Now he was a recovering control freak. He would be until the day he died. Like the recovering alcoholic, Jobs had recast his mistake as a lesson. In doing so he created a greater success than anyone had ever thought possible.

Many successful CEOs of businesses, big and small, have learned the same lesson. Mistakes are inevitable, but if you can learn from yours, mistakes can become the seeds of your success.

Brianna

That's what Brianna found out when she started her salon. By the time she was in her late twenties,

Brianna had learned the cosmetic arts of makeup and hairdressing. Since graduating from a beautician program, she'd worked in three different salons, but when she imagined opening her own, she wanted something different.

In high school Brianna had worked different jobs each summer. The last of these was at a beauty parlor, inspiring her to enroll in the local beautician school. In the previous summers she'd had jobs in a gym, and later as a salesclerk in the health food store of a health and wellness center.

Brianna talked to her friend about the features of the kind of salon she wanted to open. "I think it should combine beauty, health, and fitness," she told her friend, Connie. "So much of looking good is based in your health, and how you feel. Look at Mrs. Jackson. There she is, a thirty-five-year-old widow with three kids. You know she'd like to find a man."

"Oh, yeah. She's said so more than once," Connie agreed. "You'd think some man would give her a look.

She's strong, funny, gentle, and she always tells you where you stand. I like her."

"So do I," said Brianna. "But not many men are gonna get past all that weight. Curves are one thing, but Mrs. Jackson's shape is way past curves. If she doesn't watch herself, she's gonna turn into a mountain of fat."

"So what's that got to do with this business you're thinking of?" Connie asked.

"I think she'd be a prime customer," Brianna replied. "Look at what she does. She comes in every two weeks, gets her facial, manicure, and we style her hair. When we're done, she looks like a million bucks. She's got that smooth, creamy skin, and we make sure it glows. She's got those eyes that can light up a room. But she's also got upwards of a hundred extra pounds."

"So?"

"So, she's not gonna look her best no matter what we do. Her nice hair and that sweet, satiny complexion sit on top of a body that brings all the wrong kinds of attention. Folks laugh at that . . . and those that do the laughing aren't just insensitive men."

"I know," said Connie. "Some guys talk about liking a full-figured gal, but Mrs. Jackson is about two of those living in one body."

"Right. To really be as beautiful as she could be, she'd have to lose some weight. And we both know plenty of women just like her. That's why I'm thinking of a business that's three-in-one. First, a woman could come in, spend an hour in the gym, then maybe time in a sauna. She'd tone up all those muscles and burn off lots of fat. Then she'd come into the salon for a full treatment—hair, skin, nails, makeup—the works. Maybe we'd have a fitness specialist available. Women like Mrs. Jackson could book appointments with this specialist, and she could advise them on exercise, diet, and all the rest. We'd figure out what each client wants, and create a list. We might call it her 'beauty goals.' Then we'd help her design a program for reaching them.

"The third thing we'd have would be a health food store. If the client needed certain specialty foods we'd have them. We'd also have natural beauty products. Everything would be organic. We might even have a little café where people could get 'fitness meals.'"

"Wow! That's an incredible idea," said Connie.

Brianna smiled. "I think so, too. Now maybe I can find some folks with money they want to invest."

Brianna had saved $5,000 of her own, but she knew how inconsequential that was. It would be just enough for her to add a token financial investment to her work in starting the business. The real finances would be found elsewhere. As she began researching sites, equipment, construction costs, and leases, she realized she would need about $700,000. The number stunned her. She'd grown up thinking in terms of weekly paychecks, monthly rents, and bills that seldom came to more than a few hundred. Now she had to think about over two-thirds of a million. Yet, as she adjusted the scope of her thinking, she gained confidence, and was sure this was possible.

Brianna pinned her hopes on two of her longtime clients, Mrs. Church and Ms. Shaw. Both of these women had money, and both had talked from time-to-time about ventures in which they'd made sizeable financial investments. Brianna thought they might want to buy in, or possibly loan her the money at a better interest rate than a bank would charge. She waited for her moments, then slowly worked her way around to the subject while giving them facials. When she finally mentioned the possibility of investment, both were interested. Brianna invited both of them to Connie's apartment (which was much nicer than hers) where she'd put together a professional presentation using PowerPoint. She showed how each part of the business would work individually, and in sync with the others.

The younger of the two, Ms. Shaw, was immediately enthusiastic. "It makes so much sense," she said. "I like every part of it, and how it all fits together. I go to the gym every week, and I'm always buying health foods, supplements . . . stuff like that. And, you know, staying healthy, keeping in shape, and looking good aren't things you can really separate. Like you said, they're really all the same thing. And your idea about hiring a fitness specialist is just wonderful."

"And expensive," said Mrs. Church. A woman in her fifties, Mrs. Church had some extra pounds, and, as only Brianna knew, her natural hair color, which had gone completely white. "I think you have a good idea, but I wonder if it might not be a little too ambitious. If any part of it fails, that might bring down the whole thing. You might want to start with your strengths, then keep those other ideas on tap for expansion."

Brianna struggled to keep her disappointment from showing. "But Mrs. Church, don't you see? Each of these ideas works hand-in-glove with the others."

"That's not necessarily true," said the older woman.

"I—I think you might be looking at it the wrong way," Brianna said, struggling to focus on her argument. "You think that if one part fails, the rest will inevitably fail. I think if any of these parts work—the salon, the gym, or the health food store—all of them will work. If the gym and salon start slow, the health food store won't, or it could be any other combination. I think my best bet is the salon, and if that makes money, that's my hedge against the others taking some time before they turn a profit."

"Then why don't you start a salon instead?" Mrs. Church asked. "You could look for a location with enough room to expand. I'd be more than willing to back you in that, and if it gives you half of the seed money for the next stage, I'll match it."

"But then it's just another beauty salon," Brianna complained.

"It doesn't have to be," said Mrs. Church. "What if you had a sort of introductory version of what you're trying to do right from the start in the plan you just showed us."

"I don't get you."

"Maybe have a small exercise room off to the side, and perhaps you could sell some supplements, vitamins and non-perishable health foods, putting them all up near the register."

"But what about her fitness specialist?" asked Ms. Shaw.

"Save that for later," said Mrs. Church. "In fact, save it for last. Brianna, have you looked into what kind of salary a fitness specialist gets?"

Brianna nodded. "It's steep," she admitted. "The nationwide average is over $60,000."

"That's a whole lot of overhead, and you're locking yourself into it from the start," said Mrs. Church. "You know, most small businesses fail within a couple of years, and that's exactly the kind of monthly expense that brings them down. As you start out you want to keep your costs as low as possible. It's much easier to expand a successful business than to downsize one that's failing. You can hire your specialist when you know you have $60,000 to spend on her. Up until then you could have an agreement with one, referring interested customers to her."

"No," said Ms. Shaw. "I've seen new businesses that started on next-to-nothing. The owners are always cutting corners, and it shows. Almost all underfunded start-ups fail. You need to keep faith with your inspirations, and create your whole vision. If you do anything less, it'll never work. You've got a great idea, and I think I can guarantee that you'll find the money."

"That means $700,000 minimum," said Brianna.

"That's an awful lot of responsibility," said Mrs. Church.

"Let me talk to my banker," said Ms. Shaw. "I might be able to swing it."

Brianna looked at Mrs. Church. Despite the older woman's skepticism, Brianna felt more confidence in Mrs. Church's judgment. "Would you invest any money in my idea—meaning the whole idea?" Brianna asked.

Mrs. Church nodded. "I'd risk a little, just to have a place at the table. I wouldn't go further than $10,000. I'm rich enough for that gamble, even though I think you could have a better plan. You see, Brianna, I believe in you, but I'm not so sure you've thought it all through. In that kind of circumstance, I either turn down the opportunity, or I only invest mad money— cash on hand, that I'm not afraid to lose. That way, if the worst happens, I might invest in you again if you come up with something better. I realize you might succeed, but I'd only invest the $10,000 as a gesture from a friend."

"Don't you think I'll be her friend?" Ms. Shaw demanded.

"Maybe, but be sure you're ready for the downside of risk on your $700,000. Losing that could test any friendship. And, Brianna, if you decide to do something a little smaller and more manageable, I'd almost certainly risk more now."

"Let me think about it," said Brianna.

"That's exactly what you should do," Mrs. Church agreed.

"And when you're done thinking, let me know how you want the money," Ms. Shaw put in. "I say: Go girl! Do it now! Think big!"

Brianna considered what Mrs. Church had said. If Mrs. Church had been her only possible investor she probably would've agreed to do it her way. She saw some sense to it. "But I've thought out my idea," she told her friend, Connie. "I've worked in all three businesses, I've researched everything online, and talked to a lot of people. When Mrs. Church asked about the fitness specialist's salary, I already knew the answer. So why shouldn't I just go for it?"

"Still, from what you tell me, Mrs. Church has a point," said Connie.

"So you're with her now?" Brianna demanded.

"Honey, I'm with you. I want you to do this, and I think you can do it right, with all three parts making one big business. I'm just saying, there's something to be said for starting small, and building in stages."

"But Ms. Shaw will give me the money to do all of it—my whole vision."

"I admit, that's tempting," said Connie. "I don't know if I could turn it down. But from where I am now, it looks scary."

In the end Brianna couldn't reject the big offer. The next day she called Mrs. Church first. "I'm going to do it my way," she said. "I'm not saying you're wrong, but she's offering all the money I need, and I might never see a chance like that again."

"I understand perfectly," said Mrs. Church.

"Will you wish me luck?"

"More than that, I'd still like to be an investor. Tell me, if I were to put up $10,000, and if, by chance, something unforeseen happened, could we structure the capital in such a way that I could have the first chance to buy Ms. Shaw's shares if she ever wanted to sell them?"

"We can if it's all right with her," Brianna agreed.

Within a week lawyers had put contracts together, and the deal was struck. Brianna had $685,000 from Ms. Shaw, $10,000 from Mrs. Church, and her own tiny stake of $5,000. Still, as the CEO, all decisions were hers, and if the business succeeded she could eventually become majority owner through a formula of profit transfers.

From the start there were problems. The health food store required three different kinds of licenses. The insurance company insisted that a qualified professional always be on duty in the gym, and it would take two fitness specialists to cover all the hours. These were just two of the snags Brianna had to face. There were many more.

The gym wound up costing almost twice as much as she'd figured. That cut her operating capital to the bone. She opened with great fanfare, and got plenty of free publicity, but in the end it wasn't enough. Within months she was floundering. It looked as if Brianna's new business might not last through its first year.

When she spoke to her principal investor, Ms. Shaw was unsympathetic. "You got $700,000 from me, and what do I have to show for it?" Ms. Shaw snapped. "You said you knew what you were doing."

"I do, but you can't foresee everything. I need to do a few things differently, and that will take more money. It's not much. $20,000 would do it."

"I'm not throwing good money after bad," said Ms. Shaw. "I want out."

As Brianna left the meeting she felt an odd tingling. "I should be devastated," she thought, "yet I have a funny feeling this might be the best thing for my business."

When she talked to Mrs. Church, the older woman was both stern and comforting. "I don't have to say 'I told you so.' You already know I did. But I want to know what you've learned."

"I've learned you were right," said Brianna. "But I'm learning something else right now. I'm learning that this is the time to change things. If I don't I'll lose everything. But if I can make the right changes, I can still reach my dream. It might be a little different than I'd pictured it, but I'm learning to be more flexible. When I left Ms. Shaw I knew I should feel like crying, but I didn't. I felt like I was finally learning what I need to know."

"That's about what I hoped you'd say," said Mrs. Church. "Don't worry about Ms. Shaw. Let me call her. I'm sure we'll find a way to work things out. Start putting together a plan to streamline the business, and I'll make sure you have the chance to do it."

Six months later Brianna had managed to separate and sell off the gym as an existing business. She established a relationship with the buyers so that her clients got a special rate. She managed to keep the health food store along with the salon, which was her favorite of the three. Ms. Shaw got the cash from the sale of the gym, then Mrs. Church bought the majority of Ms. Shaw's remaining shares for $100,000. Ms. Shaw still had a 10% interest, but told her friends it was probably worthless. She was wrong.

Within a year Brianna had the business turning a profit. Three years later she bought back the gym. By that time she'd also used the original investment formula to buy 51% of her company. Mrs. Church didn't mind. "You know what you're doing now," she told her young partner. "I'll just sit back and watch my profits roll in."

Over two decades later, when Brianna's daughter, Carrie, was graduating from college, the young woman asked: "Mom, what was the most important thing you needed to know when you started the business?"

Her mother smiled. "That's easy. The thing you really need to understand is that the only way a mistake is really a mistake is when you refuse to learn from it. Whenever you mess something up, look at it as an opportunity to learn and grow. If you do that, you can't help but succeed."

SIMPLICITY: THE NAPOLEON EFFECT

Though there are several definitions of the term "The Napoleon Effect," here we are using the meaning that covers the outcomes created by methods that are as direct and simple as possible. The term for this stems from Napoleon's greatest successes on the battlefield, as he was consolidating his rule. Most of these came in his early European campaigns when his approach was to meet the enemy as quickly and directly as possible. Though sometimes outnumbered and outgunned, the charismatic general wasted little time on feints and deceits, and always pushed forward, without pause or retreat. Using the principles of simplicity and direct action, he conquered most of Europe. When he allowed his vision to blur with complications, he began to suffer defeats. Defeat led to disintegration of his army. Without a simple, unified strategy to guide him, Napoleon ultimately lost everything. His last years were spent in exile on a faraway island, where the former emperor devised ever-more circuitous stratagems for escape. None of them worked. He never regained his talent for simplicity, and never recaptured his throne.

You never have to plan complications. They always come up. A lineman stringing a wire between two poles seems to always find a tree branch or roof eave blocking his path. The dentist who's drilling a hole for a filling finds more decay than the X-ray revealed. It's always something. We have a choice between adding to these complications, or reducing them to a minimum. Adding to them piles complexity upon complexity, guaranteeing a roundabout fix that has even greater potential for trouble. Reducing them means streamlining and charting the straightest course to a solution.

Al

Al spent years learning drywall and plastering skills. Starting as a day laborer, and advancing to apprentice, then journeyman, he worked on everything from big construction projects to tiny rehab jobs. Along the way he asked questions, tried things, and developed a wide array of skills. He could wire an entire house from the basement circuit box all the way to the last outlet high in the attic. Al was a reasonably good plumber, too. He knew the ins and outs of painting, and could stud up a wall almost as fast as a good carpenter. He could tile a floor, shingle a roof, or install a heating or cooling system. So when he began to seriously plan a business where he could achieve his dreams, he thought of whole houses, not just one part of them.

"I'm gonna make myself into a general contractor," he told his friend, Ray.

Ray shook his head. "That's a lot of work, Al. When I'm on the job I watch Mr. Thornton keeping track of all that. He's always stressed and crazy."

"Yeah, but somebody's got to do it," said Al, "and that somebody's the one who counts the money."

"He might count it, but he sure doesn't get that much of it. He has to come up with our paychecks, and pay for all the materials. Then he's got the trucks, the tools, and all the expenses that go with them. And that's not even accounting for the folks at the office."

"I wouldn't have an office," said Al. "I'd do everything from my truck. I've got a laptop, and with that and a cell phone, what more do I need?"

"An accountant," Ray said.

"I'll hire one who already has his own office. I won't need a full-time accountant right away."

"Still, it sounds like a whole lot of headaches," said Ray. "Why not start a business that's based on your biggest strengths. You can do all those things, but basically you're a Sheetrock hanger and plasterer. Start doing that as a business. You can hire people, train them, and put together teams. You'd be a subcontractor on most jobs, but you'd be dealing with the skill you know better than any other. That way you're a real expert, and no one can say different."

"Too limiting," said Al. "If I'm going to build big things I gotta offer everything. I gotta be able to build whole houses—not just one part of them. It plays to my biggest strength—that I can do a little of everything."

"You can't do everything on a really big project. You need to hire lots of people, then you have to watch everything they do. You need foremen you can trust, and skilled workers who are willing to work. On a big building, you can't inspect every screw and pipe joint. You need whole crews you can count on. How would you go about hiring a whole crew?"

"The same way I hire my helpers," said Al. "I ask questions, listen to their answers, then, if that goes well, I put them on the job for a week—like a probation period. If I like what they do, they stay. If not, they go."

"Yeah, but you've never had to hire more than one at a time."

"So? I'll just teach my foremen to do what I do. Then they can do the hiring."

"But how will you decide whether to hire a foreman? You can't just put a guy you don't even know in charge of a whole job for a few days. If he's no good, you'll have a disaster."

"I'll know my foremen," said Al. "See, that's where my construction business is gonna be different. I know a few guys who are just like me. Every one of them can do everything from pouring a foundation to roofing. Each guy has the skill he specializes in, and that's what he'll concentrate on. That's how I'll split up their jobs. But they'll all have a pretty good idea of what the others are doing. They'll work better that way. Instead of having a single foreman for each project, I'll have one for each skill. An electrician will be foreman of my electrical team, a carpenter for the carpentry crew, a painter for the painting crew, and so on. Eventually I'll always have several jobs going at the same time, so a foreman might be working on more than one building at a time."

"That sounds pretty complicated," said Ray.

"No, no," Al countered. "Really it's simpler. Don't you see? These guys know all the skills, but they only have to worry about the one they're in charge of. But the fact that they know how the other stuff works will help them see how their own part of the project works in with the rest."

The following month Al finally got a general contracting license. He then presented his ideas to bankers, and found one who was willing to back him with a loan. It wasn't as much as he wanted, but he could now buy and equip four vans. One became an electrician's van, and the second was set up for plumbing work, a third was for drywall and carpentry, while the fourth had a little of everything.

His first job was building a McMansion far out in the suburbs. The customer was a brain surgeon who appreciated specialization. Al's idea about dividing crews according to skills made sense to this physician. "That's what we do in the OR," he said, "so why not on a house?"

The answer became clear almost immediately. On the first day Al arrived on the site with four foremen, each with a crew. As Al gathered everyone together, and started telling them how it would work, confusion started forming like a cloud.

"You don't even have a hole for the foundation," said the plumber. "What are me and my crew supposed to do?"

"The pipes that go through the foundation, just like you'd do on any job."

"But it's not ready for that."

"Then you and your guys help dig the foundation."

"But we're plumbers."

"That's no excuse. We all do whatever we have to do."

"Not much electrical yet," the electrician observed.

"No, but you and your guys will be wiring things up soon. In the meantime you can help when we pour the concrete."

"But that won't happen for a week," said the electrician.

"Then watch, learn, and see what you can help with, and have your guys do that, too."

"That'll make for a lot of standing around," the electrician complained.

"Yeah, well, if I see a lot of that going on, I'll find something for you to do."

The members of this oversized construction crew listened, then milled around. One team had a bulldozer, and started digging, but the others poked around trying to find something worthwhile to do. By noon Al was wondering why he'd brought in all these guys. Most were getting in the way of the few who were working. Suddenly Al clearly saw that his plan didn't work at this stage of the job. He wouldn't need most of these workers until the house was framed up.

Yet he'd committed himself. He'd promised his foremen a job and work for their crews. He'd signed contracts obligating him to make a huge payroll. Al looked out at a job site swarming with idle men, and realized he'd be broke in a week. It barely took that long.

"How could it happen?" he wondered as he was filing for bankruptcy. "The whole plan seemed so logical and right."

"Way too complicated," Ray told him. "Splitting stuff up by skill sounded good, but you forgot that all these guys have to depend on each other. When a crew is digging the foundation, they're the only ones you need. Then you bring in the concrete, and whoever's gonna work on that. You might want one plumber for intake, sewage and all that, but not enough guys to do three baths at once, with tiling and grouting included. You had an interesting idea, Al, but the main thing that made it interesting was it was so convoluted. When something's that complicated, it might appeal to folks' emotional need to try something new, but it winds up leaving most of your workers standing around. Next time you might want to try doing things in the same boring way we've always done them. Maybe the key to success in building is simply to do the same old thing the same old way, but quicker, more efficiently, and with higher quality workmanship. Simple as it sounds, that might be a smart way to do it."

"I know that now," said Al. "I was all excited, and I guess that was contagious. The money guys and the workers I hired all felt that excitement. They'd never tried something like this before. They were counting on me to know what I was talking about, but I didn't. I had passion, but I forgot to have smarts."

"I read somewhere that we all have an EQ that goes with our IQ," Ray said. "'EQ' means 'emotional quotient.' I don't know if it's a real number, like IQ, but it's all about whether we can use our emotions to our advantage, or if we let them bring us down."

"My EQ must be pretty low," Al said sadly.

"So was everybody else's. They all believed you. You've just got to work with that, and find ways to turn your emotional responses into advantages. You're smart. Make your emotions smart, too. Use your IQ to figure out the simplest way to do each task, and take emotional satisfaction from that simplicity. Whenever something looks complicated, question it. Ask whether there's a more direct way—one that gets the most out of every worker there."

"Now you tell me," said Al.

Simplicity should be easy, but it's often just as easy to overlook it. We get caught up in the intricacies of methods and systems, and forget one overwhelming truth: the shortest distance between two points is a straight line. When that line starts wandering, always ask: "Why?" And make sure you get a simple, sensible answer.

IF YOU DON'T KNOW IT, LEARN IT: BECOME A LIFELONG LEARNER

We tend to think of education in the narrow terms of school. We enter a classroom, listen to the teacher, raise our hands, ask questions, and read the textbook. We take exams, then get our report cards. If we do well, we pass through the grades, graduate, and hang a diploma on the wall. But our educations should never stop there. What we learn in school is just a foundation for everything we learn in life. The best a school can do is to teach us how to think. Day-to-day experience gives us the things to think about, and when we think, we learn.

We've talked about learning from our mistakes and failures. That's an important skill to cultivate, but we must also learn from our successes. When something goes right we have a tendency to accept the result uncritically, and go on to whatever's next. Instead we should take the time to see what we did to make the right thing happen. That way we can repeat our successes.

We should always learn from observation. Common wisdom says we learn best from experience, but observation is a kind of experience. We watch others attempt things that we've thought about trying, and see how they achieve or fail. From those observations, we tailor our own behaviors to get what we want from life. This process never ends. As long as we are alive and want to do more than eat, sleep, and breathe, we should keep learning. If we do this, our lives have the potential to always be better; if we don't, life will become empty, and we will lose all sense of purpose.

A good example of lifelong learning can be found in popular TV personality, Bill O'Reilly. When most of us think of O'Reilly, we picture the famously conservative commentator who stirs controversy with every word he utters. So to many it comes as a surprise that O'Reilly had a long, eventful television career before he went to work for Fox News in the early 1990s.

Born in 1949, O'Reilly came from a middle-class family, went to Catholic and public schools, and eventually wound up as an honors student at Marist College in New York State. He spent his junior year at the University of London. He then taught for a couple of years, and played semipro baseball, pitching for a season with the Brooklyn Monarchs, before doing graduate work at Boston University. That's when he first studied broadcasting. He spent most of the next two decades working as a TV reporter. He began on local stations, then moved up to network news. His work included a stint as a war correspondent during the Falklands conflict.

Through it all he kept learning. His job served as a continuing education. Though he always had strong opinions, he always tried to set them aside when reporting the news. This allowed him to see more than one side of many issues and situations. He covered riots, interviewed murderers, and was there for the fall of the Berlin Wall in 1989. In 1995 he took a sabbatical from TV news. He'd decided it was time to go back to school. But did this seemingly right-wing stalwart go to one of the more conservative institutions? No. He attended Harvard's John F. Kennedy School of Government. He wanted to learn more about the very institutions that drew his sharpest criticisms. When

O'Reilly talked about government, he wanted to be certain he knew what he was talking about.

In the new century, O'Reilly has made a second career for himself as the author of popular history. In recent years he's published books about the Lincoln and Kennedy assassinations.

Though his right-wing beliefs are obvious, O'Reilly is proud to say that politically he's an independent. He's an unabashed admirer of Dr. Martin Luther King and President John F. Kennedy. In his book *The O'Reilly Factor* he writes that people sometimes ask "whether I'm conservative, liberal, libertarian, or exactly what . . . See, I don't want to fit any of those labels . . . " He often seems to confirm one's suspicion that he's a conservative by railing against socialism and government spending. Yet he has also said: "Liberal thought, however, can be a good thing. Progressive programs to help the poor, fight injustice, and give people a fair shake are all positive." He surprises people, and has moments when he demonstrates curiosity and an open attitude—both essentials for lifelong learning. O'Reilly is a good example of someone who's developed the habit of learning. If you do this you can still be gaining knowledge and wisdom no matter how old you are.

Danny Wilson

Young Danny Wilson's grandpa is a good example of this. Grandpa Wilson only had a high school education, and he'd always worked in the paper mill. He could operate machinery and train newcomers, and with these skills, he always made a decent living. But as he was reaching retirement age, the paper mill closed. For the first time in his life Grandpa didn't have a job. He was old enough to qualify for Social Security benefits, and between that, and a pension, he could get by, but he was unhappy. Grandpa woke up early every morning aching for something to do.

The previous fall, when he'd still been working, Grandpa had happened to see a local ad looking for people who would deliver newspapers. Twelve-year-old Danny had been looking for paid work in the neighborhood, but had only found a weekend job walking an elderly woman's dog.

Grandpa pointed at the ad: "Delivering newspapers . . . that's what I did when I was your age."

"That's crazy," said Danny. "Kids my age never deliver newspapers. We can't."

"No?" Grandpa said, incredulous. "Why not."

"Haven't you ever seen the guy who delivers our paper?"

"No. You and your parents seem to read everything online, so I pay for the paper, but I give your mom the money, so she must be the one who talks to the boy."

"Grandpa, he's not a boy. He's Mr. Gonzalez, and he's probably as old as you are. And Mom doesn't pay him. She pays online."

"You don't say!" Grandpa exclaimed. "I'm not sure that I like that. Delivering papers is a kid's job, or it always was when I was your age."

"How could a kid deal with all those papers?" Danny asked. "It's not like we have cars. How did you do it?"

Grandpa described how papers were delivered by truck to the corner of each block. The delivery boy for that block folded them and put them in a big leather shoulder bag, then walked up the street, tossing them up at the doors. "We were supposed to 'porch it'," Grandpa said. "That meant always getting it onto the front porch where the subscriber would see it right away. When you were done with one block, more papers were waiting for you at the next one. Once a month you stopped at each house, usually in the evenings, and collected the money."

"How old were you?" Danny asked.

"Younger than you. I started when I was ten, and did it for three years, then I helped my best friend's little brother get the route. That's what kids did back then when we needed money. But if grown-ups are doing that, what kind of jobs do kids do?"

"That's what I'm trying to figure out myself," said Danny. "Every time I ask neighbors if they've got anything they need done, they say I'm too young."

Now, months later, Grandpa recalled that earlier conversation. His daughter-in-law had mentioned that Mr. Gonzalez was ending his newspaper deliveries, but she hadn't heard of anyone taking over the route. So Grandpa decided to visit their neighbor, and find out if this might be something he could do.

"The wife and I are heading for Florida," said Gonzalez. "Besides, there's fewer and fewer people subscribing to newspapers. They all get everything online. Nobody wants newspapers piling up anymore. But if you want the route, it's there. There are still some folks getting the paper, so the distributor's looking for someone to deliver it."

Grandpa got the distributor's number, and thanked Mr. Gonzalez. Then he began studying the situation. He called the distributor to find out what he should be prepared for. Danny had been right: the route was huge—far too much for a boy on foot. Then Grandpa asked Gonzalez: "Do you deliver anything but papers?"

"No. What else is there?"

"Fliers for carry-out places, neighborhood announcements, that kind of thing?"

"Nah. That's stuff people do in the afternoons. One thing I like about this job is the quitting time. We might start at three in the morning, but we're done by nine."

"I can see the advantage, though I don't mind working longer hours," said Grandpa. He was learning what he needed to know, and the wheels in his head were turning.

Grandpa then looked into the people who distributed fliers door-to-door. They worked for a statewide distribution company, which contracted with various small businesses and chains. The businesses paid the distribution company, which then had the flier printed and delivered door-to-door. Grandpa wondered why no one in town had thought of combining this with newspaper delivery.

With the paper mill closing, Grandpa knew a few other older folks who were in the same boat he was: out of work, nearing retirement age, and looking for something to do. Three of these reluctant retirees had always worked the midnight shift. All three were perfectly willing to take early-morning schedules. He also asked Danny if he was the only youngster in the neighborhood looking for paid work.

"Some of my friends have looked, but they got discouraged."

"Talk to them. See if any of them would want to get up really early and deliver papers. I think I can chop up the routes enough so they'd only work an hour or two each morning. The pay won't be that great, but if they're really interested in working, it might be more, and there could be some fringe benefits."

The biggest hurdle Grandpa faced was the law. He wanted to put preteens to work, and that was banned by child labor laws. Those laws were designed to keep unscrupulous employers from coercing children into working long hours under inhumane conditions, however, a loophole existed for paid jobs that had an educational component. That meant Grandpa would have to design it as a school-related project, get sponsorship from accredited educators, and seek school board approval. If he got that, he could make a profit, but the size and scope of the business would be regulated. Grandpa didn't mind. He wanted to make an honest dollar, and wasn't concerned with vast riches. He was in it for the challenge. If he could also do it for the children, that would be great.

He drew up a business plan that could double as a proposal for youth education. Grandpa would take over the paper route, also starting his own distribution operation for fliers. He brought in the neighborhood association, and two local nonprofits, agreeing to deliver all their handbills and announcements. He would have three retirees, each directing a delivery crew of three kids. The retirees would drop off papers at street corners, while also driving their crews to and from home. Along with the papers, they would include fliers in a special, colorful packet labeled "Neighborhood News." One of Danny's older cousins helped Grandpa set up an online payment system, and he learned to operate it. It was the first time Grandpa had ever felt comfortable online.

When Grandpa brought this plan to Danny's seventh-grade teacher, Ms. Ampalah, she liked what she saw. "I can be a sponsor for the project, and for Danny's participation in it," she said, "but you should probably get each child to find his or her own sponsor. Get those sponsors to write letters supporting your proposal. That will be a big help." This wasn't as difficult as it sounded. By the time Grandpa had all nine kids, four of them were in, or had been in, Ms. Ampalah's class. Between them the other five had three teachers who were willing to sign on. With everything in place, Grandpa took his proposal to the school board. At first the members were skeptical, but as they read, and asked questions, they began to see Grandpa's vision of a business that would bring the experience of age together with the energy of youth. They gave it conditional approval. Now he was in business!

That fall he started the newspaper routes. When winter hit, and several of the kids thought they could make extra money shoveling snow, he printed up a flier for them, and they inserted it into the "Neighborhood News" packets. Danny took over this task, and developed it into a special "Neighborhood Services" newsletter. When these listings proved to be effective, Danny started charging users a small fee.

Within a year Grandpa's business was helping over thirty local kids find paying work, while giving nine senior citizens valuable tasks that also paid reasonable wages. "I love working with these kids," said one woman. "It sure beats bagging groceries or flipping burgers." Grandpa and his fellow retirees were teaching these kids the basics of business. For some of them, including Grandpa, this was a whole new subject. Sometimes he would say: "I'm just teaching them what I'm learning. I never did this before. In the end they teach me as much as I teach them."

Though his schooling had stopped at the end of twelfth grade, the school board had officially made Grandpa into a "neighborhood educator." But Grandpa had discovered that the key to educating others was keeping your own mind open to every new idea. Without ever meaning to, Grandpa was discovering that he was a lifelong learner.

ADAPTATION: LOOKING AT WHAT'S THERE INSTEAD OF WHAT'S NOT

Into every life some rain must fall, and every job has its rough patches. It's easy to get angry and discouraged. But if you give up at the first sign of trouble, you won't get anywhere. Always focus on what you have, and if you can't get something you need, look for the best substitute. Often you'll find something as good or better as whatever it was you thought you needed.

Adaptation is the ruling principle here. As we've already seen, one of the world's greatest innovators of the last century, Steven Jobs, learned to be a master of adaptation. When he found himself in trouble, he learned fresh approaches and new skills. When he was turned out of his own company, he looked for something that could stir his passion in an entirely new area: digital animation and graphics in movies.

Jobs' biggest rival in the digital world was Bill Gates, founder and longtime owner of Microsoft. Gates had built his company on the success of DOS, a pioneering computer operating system that had been adopted by IBM. When PCs became popular, opening up a vast untapped market of potential users, Gates saw the need for a more intuitive operating system. He adapted, and the result was Windows.

Windows systems operate according to the principle of adaptation. Users can open most files and programs in several different ways. You might access something by clicking on its icon, but if that doesn't work, you can right click on the same icon, and get a menu with an "Open" option. If you search around, you'll find several other methods for performing this most basic task. When his rival, Jobs, saw the first version of Windows, he knew his former company, Apple, and other digital giants would have to adapt. They did, and today many users feel that Mac and Linux systems make Windows even better.

Jobs learned to do his best with whatever was at hand. He didn't get angry; he got creative. When you get frustrated, look at the tools you have, think of them creatively, and apply this same method of thinking to your goal. You will find a way!

Janice Mays

Janice Mays had to learn the skills of adaptation the hard way. She'd just gotten her degree in media studies from her local community college when tragedy struck her family. Her dad died of a sudden heart attack, leaving her with the responsibility of deciding what to do with the family business, an old-style corner grocery store in a city neighborhood. Janice had come up dry in her first job search, so she was faced with a choice: either try to run the store and turn a profit, or sell it for whatever they could get.

The store took up the front of the first floor of the building. The back was a complex maze of small rooms where Mr. Mays kept an office, backup merchandise, and storage space for all the junk a family collects over a lifetime. The family occupied the second and third floors. Though Janice had twin brothers, Willie and Fred, neither of them had the time or inclination to deal with the family business. Willie had chosen a career in the Navy, while Fred had a good job with Social Security. Almost a decade younger, Janice still lived at home. She'd been working in the grocery store part-time since middle school. Her dad had never pressured her to stay on, but he had taught her the basic chores for running it. She was the only one in a position to make informed decisions about it.

"Couldn't we just sell it?" asked her mom. Through decades of bringing up her family, Mrs. Mays had seldom paid much attention to the store downstairs. To her it was a handy source of groceries, but little more.

"We couldn't get much for it right now," said Janice. "These last couple of years the store's barely broken even, and with a new supermarket, and that chain convenience store that just opened up, prospects aren't good. We might do better just to sell off the stock and equipment, then close."

"It's so sad," said Mrs. Mays. "It'll be sixty years next summer since your grandparents opened this store. Your father remembered the day they opened. He was six years old. He used to think one of your brothers would want it, but they have their own lives, I guess."

"I could take it over," said Janice. "Dad taught me what to do. Maybe I can turn it around, and then maybe we can get a little cash selling it."

"I suppose that's what your father hoped," said Mrs. Mays.

For the first couple of weeks Janice did things exactly as her dad had taught her. Each morning she counted out $150 in cash and coins for the register. She did inventory once a week, and made up orders on Monday and Tuesday for end-of-the-week delivery. She did the banking, paid the bills, and tallied up the results each night. Her tallies weren't always encouraging.

"How did Dad manage it?" she often wondered.

When it became clear that she would be doing this for a while, Janice began studying the retail grocery field. She found a couple of booklets and websites covering small grocery businesses. Most modern ones were convenience stores that were franchised by nationwide chains. The number of independents was plunging. Still, the more she learned, the more Janice thought that her family's store had potential.

She visited other independents, talked to managers of the chain stores, and looked for ideas that might attract an audience. When she asked neighbors what they liked best about her store, they spoke of service, convenience, but most of all they talked about how well it fit the neighborhood. "I see my friends in here," said one elderly man. "After school I find my girlfriends here, or right out there on the sidewalk," said a twelve-year-old girl." Her mother added: "Because you're here, I always know where to start looking for her. Usually I find her right back there, reading your magazines."

Janice began to focus on something she'd always taken for granted: the store was a hub for a lot of activity that had little to do with groceries. Neighbors met neighbors in the aisles, and many residents had been making a stop at the store a part of their daily routine for years. Now and then someone would ask to post a flier for something: a school activity, or apartment for rent, or yard sale. Her grandparents, and later her father, had always had a policy of not posting anything. There had probably been a reason for this once, but now the policy was more a matter of habit than anything else. Janice now realized that this was a policy she should change.

She put up two cork bulletin boards, one inside the store, and one outside for casual foot traffic. She explained that the outdoor bulletin board was for public activities, while the one inside was for more personal messages. "If you're interested in buying or selling something, or you want people to know about a job you do, or need done, or a service you provide, or want, put your notice on the indoor board. If you're putting something up that's nonprofit, or personal, or you're posting an open message for the neighborhood, like for a school play, or a church bizarre, all those go outside. That way the personal service fliers are in here, where anyone can ask me about the people posting them; and people can read the more general, public messages out there anytime, even when we're closed."

It was a small gesture, yet Janice quickly noticed that the message boards brought in business. When the boards filled, she added extra sections, then organized them into categories. One board had nothing but offerings of apartments and houses, and postings from people who were looking for somewhere to live. Another covered church, school, and charity events. One board was full of personal notices, including romantic and humorous appeals. Janice monitored these closely to weed out any she found questionable. She was surprised at all the interest.

"It's so local and personal," said Mr. Davis, who taught high school math. "You have those kinds of postings on internet sites like Craigslist, but they're citywide, with national ads mixed in. No one really monitors them. But when I see something on your bulletin boards, I know it was almost certainly posted by a neighbor. I can ask you who they are, and you'll probably know. I can meet the person here, where I know I'm safe. For neighborhood contacts it's much better than the web."

Janice thought about his comments, and started looking through the densely-packed warren of storage rooms in the back. Most of the rooms were filled from floor to ceiling. Even the sizeable office barely allowed space for a desk, two chairs, and a file cabinet. The rest of the room was junk piled on junk.

When Janice asked her mom about this, Mrs. Mays replied: "I never look at that stuff. I know if I do I'll try to keep everything, even though I know we should get rid of it. So I don't even want to look at it. As far as I'm concerned you should just hire someone to haul it to the dump. That way I'll never miss it."

"There might be a better solution," Janice said.

"That's fine, but don't bother me with it," said her mom.

That gave Janice what she needed: permission. Starting into the first room, she unearthed three childhood dolls of her own, and some of her brothers' sports equipment. Once she was past the basketballs, baseball bats, and lacrosse sticks, she was faced with endless bags of clothes, discarded furniture, and at least two broken air conditioners.

That afternoon she got on the phone to her brothers. "There are big piles of stuff in storage here, and I need to move it elsewhere," she said. "A lot of it is yours. If you don't want it, fine. I can give it to Goodwill or sell it. But if you want to look through it first, come by anytime this weekend." That brought both brothers to the store. Janice showed them what she was trying to do in the back rooms.

"Why do we have to do this now?" asked Willie, staring at the impossible task.

"I want this space," she said. "The store could be much bigger, or this could become a lunchroom."

"You're getting ambitious," said Fred.

"I thought it was just good sense," she countered. "If anybody's ever going to pay what this business is worth, I have to make it look good."

She hurried them along in their efforts to identify what should be saved, and what should be discarded. One brother found a treasure trove of baseball cards.

The other discovered their grandparents' 78rpm records from the 1940s. Janice encouraged them to get something out of their finds.

"You should sell anything you don't want," she said. "You could eBay just about all of this stuff."

"I don't have the time," said Willie.

"Yeah," said Fred. "I don't know if it would be worth the hassle. Better to just haul it all to the dump. If you want to arrange that, I'll pay for my part."

"So would I," said Willie.

"And if I can sell it?"

Both men laughed. "If you can sell any of this stuff, we should get half," said Willie.

"How about a quarter?"

"That's fi—" Fred started.

"Half," Willie snapped, cutting off his brother.

"A quarter is all I'm offering," said Janice. "I'll be the one doing the work you don't want to do. If you want to sell it yourselves, be my guest. If not, either I will sell it for you, and take the lion's share of profit, or it goes to the dump." After a few more minutes of sparring with her brothers, she had the deal she wanted.

Janice used her own bulletin boards to advertise for kids who knew their way around eBay. She found three high school students who were willing to give up their Saturday mornings in return for another 25% from any eBay sales. She would still get half. First they helped her separate the collectibles from the dross. The kids proved their value in this task. To them none of these items were personal, so they were never slowed by nostalgia. They made a pile of everything worth selling, and a second pile for Goodwill or the dump.

Once they'd cleared the first small room, Janice looked over the items slated for sale, and saw quite a few that a grocery store might stock. In the newly cleared room she set up a table and a display case. She cleaned and polished up each item, then priced them at about what they might bring at a yard sale. Once she'd set them out in attractive arrangements, she put up a sign over the room's entrance pointing potential customers inside. The sign read: "Our Old Becomes Your New!"

The results pleased her. Working from a PC in the store's office, her high school kids managed to rake in over $7,000 total, with Janice getting half. Their piles of sale items shrank, and finally almost disappeared. Janice learned that the things that sold best there in the store were items that had become memorabilia from the neighborhood and region. Anything with a local angle went quickly, and for top dollar. Most of the other items just sat until she handed them over to her young helpers for disposal.

They did this with each room and section, refining and adapting sales techniques, presentation, and pricing. After six months the storage areas were cleared, and Janice had a total profit of $16,000 from this "junk." She paid her brothers, then the kids, then she used the rest as a part of the financing for a renovation. Within a year after she'd taken over the grocery, Janice had knocked down the walls in the back, making one big room, and doubling her space.

As of today she's put in a small kitchen, along with tables and chairs, creating a diner where customers can get breakfast or lunch. She's doing good business, but she's learned that in her neighborhood there's not much demand for diner-style meals during the dinner hour. That's inspired her to let community organizations use this new space for evening events and meetings. On Friday nights a nearby church sponsors a coffeehouse for teens. Janice also hosts Boy Scouts, Girl Scouts, and board meetings of the neighborhood association. All of this attracts more customers than Janice thought possible.

Now neighborhood residents see the old corner grocery as the new community center. Janice is so busy, and so successful, that she hardly even thinks about any other possible jobs she might have. She feels she could be happy doing this kind of thing for the rest of her life.

The key to Janice's success is adaptation. Every time she identifies a problem, she immediately looks for creative ways to fix it. She always looks at the problem within the whole context of her store, including everything that's already in it. There are usually a number of solutions. That's when Janice asks herself: What measure can I take? Which ones best fit with the business I have now? Which solution has the most positive potential?

She's learned that adaptation is the main ingredient in any recipe for recovery, rejuvenation, and success. You can do the same with any task you take on.

IF YOU DON'T HAVE IT, GET IT: BE PREPARED

E ffort is a key to any enterprise. While it's true that if you don't try you will never fail, you won't succeed, either. Success comes only to those who make a real effort. The most effective efforts are those that are backed up by proper preparation.

Successful boxers are models of preparation. The great Floyd Mayweather has come back from adversity, and won multiple world boxing titles, by preparing himself thoroughly for each bout. He knows that every knockout punch is preceded by hours, days, and weeks of practice.

Mayweather owns more crowns in more weight divisions than any professional boxer in history.

Experts have rated him the best boxer fighting today pound-for-pound. He comes from a family of boxers. His uncles have both won important fights and championships, while his father earned a bout with the great Sugar Ray Leonard.

Despite all this, young Mayweather had a difficult youth. His father dealt drugs, both of his parents were addicts, and one aunt died from AIDS. Young Floyd grew up in an atmosphere of drugs and violence.

Through most of Floyd's teenage years his father was in prison. This was when the young man built himself into one of the nation's top ring prospects. To him this was a matter of necessity. With his dad gone, it fell upon Floyd to support his mom. To do this he quit school, and spent most of his days at the gym, preparing. In the career that followed he was 84-6 as an amateur, and, as of this writing (summer of 2013) he remains undefeated after seventeen years as a pro.

Mayweather's signature trait is preparation. He knows what goes into every punch, every step, and every feint. He trains long and hard for all contingencies. Even between training periods he keeps himself in shape. His trainers have said that Mayweather is probably ready to fight after just a few days of his regular training regimen—but he takes six weeks, and covers everything repeatedly.

"One of the things that amazes me . . . about Floyd is that he works and trains like he never made a dime," says his friend and business partner, Leonard Ellerbe. "It's incredible . . . pushing himself the way he does. He's a perfectionist." After witnessing one of the boxer's recent training sessions, Yahoo columnist, Kevin Iole wrote: "Mayweather frequently pushes himself beyond normal limits, as if he were an 18-year-old hoping to catch the eye of a local promoter, not the biggest star in boxing on the homestretch of his career." It's an attitude that has made Mayweather the richest athlete on the planet.

Mayweather is an almost perfect example of the value of proper preparation. He trains hard so he can fight hard, concentrating entirely on the moment in the ring, and his opponent. He knows that a good training program that tries to cover every possibility will always miss something. But that training also unlocks his mind, so that he has the tools to create a response to any new situation.

That's what we have to do if we're going to win in business.

Ron and Dave

The experiences of two friends, Ron and Dave, show how essential good prep work is. These two went through school together, then both took jobs at a local manufacturing company. Twelve years later, when the company needed to downsize, it offered both of them generous buyouts. They thought of going into business together, but each of them wanted to do different things. Knowing they wouldn't be competing with each other, they agreed to start their businesses, and if either one failed, he could get a job working for the other.

Ron started a restaurant, while Dave began a men's clothing store. Ron chose a restaurant simply because he liked to cook and eat. At the beginning those were his only qualifications. Dave decided on men's clothing because he'd worked in his uncle's clothing store through high school and college. He knew the business.

Ron appreciated his own lack of experience, and approached his venture carefully. Over the next six months he read everything he could find on restaurant operations. He took two courses, one in food prep, and the other in small business management. He went out to different restaurants all the time, never eating at home. He asked owners, chefs, and staffers questions. What gets done before opening? How many waitstaff for how many tables? Where could he get the best meats? Or produce? Or micro-brewed beer?

Ron took his time searching for the right location. He wanted to be on a corner, and he wanted enough room to feed one hundred people. He hoped to find a place that already had some equipment. He also looked into what it would cost to buy state-of-the-art fixtures.

Dave wasn't as thorough. He felt like he already knew the basics, so he only had to fill in details. He read little, talked to no one, and rented the first retail space he could find. It had been a record store, but that had gone out of business five years earlier. The place had been vacant through the economic downturn.

Once Ron found a good location he cultivated local food critics and bloggers. He put together his own website with room for a menu, and a contact link for reservations and catering. He found a good chef, and let the man hire his own kitchen crew. Ron then hired a floor manager, and together they put together a waitstaff and bartenders. Working with these colleagues, Ron designed his floor plan. He did it carefully, but left room for changes, should they be necessary. All of his plans were consistent, yet flexible. He knew that many restaurants needed several months to perfect their operations, so he met with investors to make sure he had adequate capital. The night Ron opened he watched everything, making constant notes. By morning he was already busy tweaking his operations.

Within a month Ron's place was getting excellent reviews. His business started slowly, but the volume grew a little each week. In his fourth month he broke even. By the end of his first year he could boast that he'd already made a small profit. By the end of his second year his restaurant was considered to be one of the best in the city. By that time he'd given Dave a job as a bartender.

Dave had been in trouble from the beginning. He hadn't lined up much capital, so he could only do so much renovation. Many of the record store's fixtures remained, and he used them to display merchandise.

Fine shirts and dress slacks looked out of place in converted CD bins. He opened without any full lines of brands. Instead he had only what he could afford with his meager capital. When he advertised for two sales assistants, none of the applicants had experience. He figured he'd train the two he hired, but he soon realized he didn't know how to train workers. He'd never had to do it before.

People who came in often left saying the same thing: "This guy's an amateur." Sales were fair the first week, bad the first month, and in three months Dave closed his doors. Luckily he'd sometimes moonlighted as a part-time bartender, so when he went to Ron he had a skill to fall back on. Ron hired him and gave him good shifts. Dave turned out to be a much better bartender than he'd been a clothing store manager. Maybe all he needed was a boss.

Later that year, when Ron's nephew emailed him saying he was going to start his own business, he asked his uncle for advice. Ron wrote back:

"With any business certain things apply: hard work, good sense, and proper preparations. The key is to motivate yourself. Do this by setting goals that you truly want to reach. Prepare yourself for starting your business by gathering whatever resources you need. Figure out what you want to do. Identify the necessary tasks, then list the items and actions you need to perform those tasks. Get the items, and prepare yourself to take action. Don't rest until you see your first profit."

Truer words were never written.

HOW TO AVOID FRUSTRATION— FORGET ABOUT WHAT YOU DON'T HAVE AND FOCUS ON WHAT YOU DO

W e all want a perfect world, but it never happens. When you start a business, you have a picture of it in your mind. That picture is your perfection. As always, the reality will be considerably different. Flaws are inevitable. If you can't operate a flawed enterprise, you're probably not yet ready to start your own business. Such an attitude will lead to frustration, and, inevitably, failure. The solution is a new application of a principle we've already seen: adaptation. This time you concentrate on adapting to reality, and accepting certain limitations:

forget about the impossible, and concentrate on what you can do with what's actually there.

Sam Su and KFC

One great example of this kind of adaptation in the business world is the experience of Kentucky Fried Chicken in the Chinese market. In the 1960s and 1970s, KFC was one of the fastest growing of all the fast-food chains. They spread across America's landscape along with the interstates, providing easy, fast meals to people on the road. By the 1980s they were moving into the international marketplace, bringing buckets of "finger lickin' good" chicken to countries all over the world. In 1987 they opened their first locations in China.

When parent company Yum! Brands formed KFC's China division they appointed Taiwanese-born Sam Su to be its CEO. Su soon realized that KFC's standard American business model wouldn't work in China. It was a different culture with different values, and any large foreign enterprise would have to adapt to succeed. Part of the difference lay in culture and psychology. "There's no room for ego," Su explains. "China doesn't have the same culture of individualism that is present in the U.S."

He didn't strip out everything American. Su says that instead it was a matter of taking "the best ideas from the U.S. fast-food model and adapt[ing] them to serve the needs of the Chinese consumer." This was his criteria when he hired his team. He hired local Chinese managers who knew the language and culture, but who were also familiar with Western business practices. "[T]hey also understood the challenges of operating in this Chinese, very traditional, very evolving market," write KFC chroniclers David Bell and Mary Shelman.

In everyday business, Su created a corporate atmosphere based more in internal camaraderie than competition. The people in KFC China operation got along. They were informal, talking to each other like members of a happy family. This casual attitude at the top filtered down through managers and staffers in KFC outlets throughout China.

Chinese workers had a different set of priorities, which created attitudes more in keeping with their culture. In the less affluent culture of late twentieth-century China, managers were expected to understand that workers had many obligations pulling at them. If a student's academic duties came into conflict with his or her work schedule, the schoolwork always won. A manager only asked to be given enough notice so that others could be assigned the extra workload.

During breaks young employees were encouraged to gather together and mingle. The company provided video games for workers to play during breaks, while sponsoring many other social activities. Most of these workers were teens still living at home. The company's policies eased their parents' minds. In most cases this was the first time their children had worked for a Western company, and parents were reassured by the company's concern about its workers' well-being and social habits.

Su also realized that KFC's standard practice of developing through a standard franchising model wouldn't necessarily work in China. In most parts of the world, KFC (and most other international fast-food chains) spread through a method of establishing regions, then setting up separate franchises which would be run by their owners. Each franchise would operate on its own, something like an independent business. One roadblock to this in China was the distribution systems. The nation lacked nationwide third-party supply systems, so KFC set up its own, which meant everything would be more centralized.

Su also used Chinese food vendors as much as possible. Unlike the U.S., with its huge poultry operations, this often meant going to individual Chinese farmers, each of whom might only be supplying as little as a few birds per week. He built his supply chain from the ground up. This allowed him to adapt inspection systems so the safety record of his products is far better than most in China.

The products themselves are evidence of the marriage of cultures. A Chinese KFC menu features American staples such as mashed potatoes and crispy bone-in fried chicken. But Chinese patrons also love the shrimp burgers and soymilk drinks.

The result is an object lesson in adaptability. KFC China is still KFC, but no one would mistake it for its American counterpart. Many of its signature aspects originated here, but if a Western business practice went against the Chinese grain, Su and his team changed it. Over a quarter century later they've created a legendary success story.

Wanda

The principle of adaptation worked on much smaller scales, too. A good example of this comes from another food business, this one tiny. Thirty-one-year-old Wanda owned and operated her food truck for nearly five years. She served chili, hot dogs, burgers, chicken, fries—most of the fast lunch staples. Though her meals were a little pricier than those found at most food trucks, Wanda concentrated on high-quality meats and creative specials to create more value. She found people were willing to pay extra for a better meal. She moved around, using a half dozen locations, depending on the time of year.

She'd done well, and as she watched her business increase she considered expansion. At first she thought about a second truck, but the obstacles seemed daunting. A second mobile unit would mean training someone to manage a truck, and hiring an extra assistant. If an emergency arose in the second truck, Wanda wouldn't be there to handle it. One of the best places for her second truck to operate would be in the suburban office complex just outside the city limits. That meant a different jurisdiction, which would bring extra costs, inspection concerns, and a new set of licensing requirements.

For a while that's where her thinking stopped. She knew she could do it, but she couldn't decide whether to take the risk. Then something happened that shook up her plans. Her best current location was a downtown street corner where she parked for two months in mid-winter and two months in mid-summer. It had been her first spot. She could've parked there all year and made a profit, and she'd debated doing just that. But she recognized there would be a trade-off: if she eliminated her truck's visits to other areas, she would lose a lot of her visibility, and her overall sales might suffer.

Across the street from her downtown spot sat a vacant retail space. It had once been an open-air grill, serving a menu something like her own, but six years earlier they had a fire and closed. The building's owners had never gotten around to repairing the damage. At first they'd shown it to prospective renters, offering a deal to share the cost of renovation. When Wanda was first thinking of starting a business, she'd taken a tour of the facility. There was storage space, an auxiliary cooking area in the back, and the storefront with its counters and windows opening out on the street. It was a good setup, but the deal the owners were offering wasn't so great. Any new tenant would have to pay all renovation costs. Like other possible renters, Wanda turned it down.

Recently the building had changed hands. The new owner was a Realtor who often ate his lunch at Wanda's truck. When she asked him his plans for the grill, he said: "Wanda, I'd hate to rent to your competition, so maybe I can interest you. Would you want to set up something permanent that wasn't on wheels?"

She told him of the earlier owners' offer, and why she'd turned it down. "I was just starting out," she said, "and if I'd gone in there it would've cost a whole lot more than fitting out this truck."

"What if I can offer you something better than they did?" the new owner asked.

Wanda thought about it for a moment. "I guess I'd be willing to listen," she conceded.

The new owner was already starting renovations on the whole building. He was willing to tailor the work his crew did on the grill to Wanda's needs. "I won't do all your work for you," he said, "but I can leave whatever you want, and if you need to have something removed, or a wall torn down, I can do that. I'll also go half with you on plumbing and electrical, but only if you're willing to sign a long-term lease."

Wanda had to think about this. Most of it was better than the previous offer, but she was hesitant about the long-term lease. In five years she'd gotten used to owning her own place of business, and a mobile one at that. She could pick up and move her location at a moment's notice. Now she was faced with the question of whether she could handle being tied to a particular spot all year.

The new owner sweetened the deal, offering to pay for all her new plumbing fixtures. That, combined with the fact that this was already her best sales location, persuaded Wanda, and she finally agreed. She was nervous, but she felt she could see a clear avenue to success. She would keep her truck. She would supply it from the grill, and sometimes go out with it herself. She could scout new locations for mid-winter and mid-summer, looking for places that promised good sales and high-profile exposure. She wanted her truck patrons to come to the grill whenever they were downtown.

The road to success had some bumps. She promoted her assistant, Bill, to run the truck operations, but he wasn't ready for the workload. She sat him down, talked it out with him, and, once he got over his fear of getting fired, he admitted he was in over his head. "Bill, you're a good assistant manager," she said, "and I still haven't found a permanent assistant for the grill. The hours would be shorter, and

I'll be there to help you with staff, inventory, and the rest." Relieved, he agreed. Six months later they were both happy with the results. Wanda then hired a truck manager, Vickie, who'd once had her own food truck. Vickie increased sales, and within a few months was urging Wanda to expand to two trucks. "That was my original thought," Wanda said, "and now, if you can manage them both, I'll do it." Vickie readily agreed.

Wanda now had a much bigger kitchen to run. At first it seemed overwhelming, but through trial-and-error she gradually assembled a good kitchen crew. As she went along she learned what questions to ask prospective employees, as well as what to listen for in their answers. She wanted people who knew what they were doing, but were always open to new ideas. She was looking for the thing she'd found in herself: adaptability.

After three years, Wanda has a smooth-running operation. From her lone assistant, her staff has expanded to fifteen employees. Her main location thrives year-round, and her trucks spread the experience of her meals throughout the region. Both trucks are moneymakers, and she plans to add a third one soon.

Wanda has learned the same thing Sam Su did in China: Every task can be done by a variety of methods. The right one for one circumstance may be wrong for another. When you're facing a new situation, look at the tools you have, think of them creatively, and apply this thinking to your goal. You will find a way!

TAKE RESPONSIBILITY

When things go wrong, many people run for cover. That's not what an employer wants when he hires you, nor will it help you run a business. When working for others, you must accept responsibility for anything you do on the job. When you risk everything you have on a business, you must accept responsibility no matter what the outcome. If you're always ready to run away from your failures, you'll have a much harder time getting credit for your achievements.

Oprah

One person who's always accepted her responsibilities is the most famous woman on earth:

Oprah. Oprah's life began in such poverty that she often had to wear dresses her grandmother sewed together from old potato sacks. Born to an unwed teenaged mother, she grew up moving between several different homes. As a child she suffered from sexual abuse, and when she was thirteen she ran away from home. Not long after that her mother sent her to live with her father. He was stern, but caring, and as Oprah went through high school her talents began to emerge. She won a scholarship to college after winning an oratory contest. Oprah then won a pageant crown as Miss Black Tennessee, and soon started her career in broadcasting.

When Oprah first worked as a TV reporter on local stations in Nashville and Baltimore, she had to do the jobs she was told to do. Often this meant putting her dreams on hold. She recognized this, and accepted it. She was a thorough reporter and a talented anchor. She took full responsibility for every story she aired. At the same time she never lost sight of her larger goals. She did her job well, impressed those who were in a position to help her, and kept her eyes on the prize: she wanted to succeed in television and have her own show under her control.

Oprah was still in her twenties when she first moved to Chicago. She'd already done well in her earlier jobs, and now she saw the opportunity she needed: a daytime talk show. It was AM Chicago. When Oprah took it over the show was suffering from the lowest rating in its time slot. That's when she began shaping the style that would make her famous. Though her questions weren't terribly tough, and she avoided confrontations, her welcoming attitude encouraged her guests to open up. Often they said things they would've never uttered to any other interviewer.

In a few short months the ratings for AM went from last to first place, even beating the Chicago-area ratings of her soon-to-be-rival, Phil Donahue. Within three years she went national. This pitted her against

Donahue coast to coast. Her show skyrocketed to the top of the ratings.

In that first incarnation, her show pioneered a format that was coming to be known as "tabloid TV." This was a genre marked by real people airing their real conflicts with one another. Family members accused each other of abuse or wrongdoing. There was often a lot of sexual subject matter in the mix, as well as violence. Oprah herself revealed on TV that she'd been the victim of sexual abuse as a child.

Though she helped invent the "tabloid TV" format, Oprah never engaged in the kind of sensationalism some other talk shows thrived on. She sincerely tried to settle differences, calm waters, and encourage emotionally fragile guests to heal. In the mid-1990s she redesigned her format, stepping away from on-air confrontations, and focusing instead on a mix of topical issues and in-depth interviews with many of the world's best-known celebrities, usually featuring questions about the causes they were promoting. In the next fifteen years she conversed with such public figures as Michael Jackson, David Letterman, Sarah Palin, and many more.

Her show was only the most visible of an incredible array of enterprises. Oprah acted (*The Color Purple, The Women of Brewster Place*, etc.), produced (her own show, TV movies, and a stage version of *The Color Purple*), and published her own monthly magazine. Not only did she become the world's most successful media personality, but she also amassed a fortune in the billions. By the time she wrapped up her TV show in 2011 (after a twenty-five-year run) she was the most famous woman on the planet.

Through her career Oprah has drawn criticism. Journalists complained that her interviews were shallow and self-serving for her guests. They say she didn't probe, and tread lightly in areas where her guests preferred not to go. Her supporters countered that her sympathetic style permitted her guests to open up, leading them to talk more freely. Some critics discounted her interest in book features, saying her recommendations were too middle-of-the-road. Yet others would argue that her reading list was accessible and substantive, and encouraged many TV viewers to finally turn off the set and open a book.

Oprah has never hidden. It's one of the secrets of her success. She always accepts responsibility for her decisions, often doing so quite publicly. She admits errors, corrects them, learns from them, and moves on. That's a good lesson for any job seeker or entrepreneur.

If you want to succeed on the deepest level, you must have respect for yourself and the actions you take. That means taking responsibility for both the good and the bad. After a few years of hosting her tabloid show, Oprah realized that she'd reached the limits of that format. Her critics had a point: she could do better, more essential work in television. She didn't have to change. Her show's ratings were still the best in all of daytime television. Her sponsors were happy, her viewers loved her, and her other ventures were thriving. But Oprah knew things had to change. It was time for something different. She revised her format, attracted fascinating guests, and began exerting influence on everything from popular culture to politics. By the time Barack Obama began his run for the presidency, Oprah was in a position to be one of his key allies. That's just one of the rewards she earned from taking responsibility for her actions.

Justin and Malik

The principle of taking responsibility applies to small ventures, too. Justin and Malik graduated from high school together. Malik got a job with a painting company, while Justin studied business and accounting at the community college. After his first year in college, Justin took a summer job with Malik's company. Justin didn't have enough for his second year tuition, so he signed up for a single night class, and spent his days painting. Both boys stayed at home, keeping their expenses to a minimum. A year later he and Malik each had over $5,000 saved.

Both young men were skilled painters, and both had dreams. Malik shared his goals with Justin.

"I want to start my own painting business," Malik said. "I know how to talk to the customers, price the jobs, and organize the work. If we did it together, you could keep the books, do the payroll, and write the checks. We could pool our money, get a used truck, ladders, harnesses, and all the other gear."

"How big a crew are you thinking about?" Justin asked.

Malik shrugged. "We could start with just you and me. We could handle anything up to an average-sized house. If we get something bigger, and we're pressed for time, we can always hire extra people. I even know of a job that's coming up—one we could get. My Uncle Charlie needs a building painted. It's a big garage—fits four cars—with two apartments above it. We'd be painting inside and out. You can look at it with me, and see what you think, but it should pay about $7,000 for the labor. I haven't figured out materials yet. Anyway, we could start on that, then see if anything develops."

Though Justin had planned to return to school, he liked his friend's idea. Justin already understood basic bookkeeping, and he knew how to calculate the bottom line. He talked about it with his dad, who was positive, but cautious.

"Remember," Justin's dad said, "when you own your own business, your reputation is on the line with everything you do. If you screw up, you're responsible. The same goes for your employees. Are you going to paint interiors?"

Justin nodded. "Of course. We'll paint indoors or outdoors."

"Then you'll need bonding two ways."

"Even while it's just the two of us?"

"Yes," said Justin's dad. "You're probably safe painting that garage without insurance, but you'll need it to get a business license. People like to know a company is safe. A surety bond insures your work. If you don't fulfill your obligations, the company bonding you will pay your customer. When you start hiring employees you'll want a fidelity bond. That will protect you and your customer against employee theft and potential damage."

"But we don't even have any employees."

"So you probably won't need the fidelity bond right away, but once you start working for strangers, the surety is a must. It could be a good test for both of you. Tell Malik you'll start with him on his uncle's building, but make sure he commits to saving enough for the business license and surety bond. Each of you should set aside half that cost from your pay from the garage work. If you already have capital for the rest, then doing this should get you started. If you need someone to cosign anything, or vouch for you, I'll do it, but only if both of you have shown you can finance this yourselves."

"That makes sense."

That afternoon Justin did research online, then made some calls. He learned that a license and a reasonable surety bond would cost about $1,500. The next day Justin suggested his dad's plan to Malik.

"Why would we need a bond?" Malik asked.

"It's insurance," said Justin. "We would post it on our truck, and use it in our advertising. If people know we're bonded they feel they can count on us. And if we're going to get licensed, we have to get the bond. The state requires it."

"I know a lot of guys who work for themselves, but they don't have any bonds, licenses, or any of that stuff."

"Yeah, but they're not running real businesses that can grow. To do that, they would have to be licensed and bonded."

"Okay, okay, I'll do it," Malik conceded. "How much do we need?"

"$750 each," said Justin. "Not even a quarter of what we'd get paid for the garage work. It should be easy."

"Yeah," said Malik. "Easy."

Two weeks later they started work. Though they'd done the final pricing together, Malik took over the business end. "Uncle Charlie's my relative," he explained. "He'll be more comfortable talking money with me. I'll keep you up to date on everything."

With both of them working overtime, it took them three weeks. Each week Uncle Charlie gave Malik a check, then Malik paid his friend in cash.

"We won't be able to do it that way once we're licensed," Justin warned him. "We'll need to have paychecks, withholding—all that."

"I know," Malik said. "Once that happens, you'll do the accounting."

When they finished, Malik went to his uncle, but this time he came back empty-handed. "Uncle Charlie will pay us next week," he said.

"Okay, but we'll have to make our regular customers pay on time," Justin said.

"I know that."

"Next week" became the week after that, then the week after that. Finally, after a month, Malik gave Justin most of the pay due him. "It's a couple of hundred short," Malik said, "but I gave him a break because he's family. I'll make it up to you on the next one."

Justin took the money, and said: "I guess I'll have to take it, and I can probably still come up with my half of the bond and license fees."

Malik hesitated. "Yeah, well, about that . . . I'm not quite there yet. Why don't we do another job like this one? Then I'll have enough."

"Have you got a job in mind?"

"Let me check into it."

That night Justin told his dad everything that had happened. "What should I do?" he asked.

"If you want to do another job with him, go ahead, but get him to pay you in advance, a week at a time. And, while I know he's your friend, don't go into business with him. This was the test. He failed it. That means he's not ready for the responsibility, and that's what the licensing and bonding are all about."

Justin took his dad's advice. He worked three more jobs with Malik, then his friend failed to come up with a week's pay, and the two parted ways. But by that time Justin had saved enough to start his own painting business. He started small, made mistakes, and learned from them. Soon his business grew. He got his license, bought both bonds, and hired his first employees. Soon his business thrived. Meanwhile Malik kept taking small jobs, and often had trouble collecting his pay.

Justin had grasped the lessons of responsibility. His customers appreciated this, and almost always paid on time. The benefits of taking responsibility come slowly, but they serve as a foundation for solid success.

THE KIM KARDASHIAN EFFECT:
SELF-CONFIDENCE SPELLS SUCCESS

Kim Kardashian

You might think she's crazy, selfish, bizarre, or inane, but it's hard to turn on a TV or surf the net without running into Kim Kardashian. Her celebrity grows out of relentless self-promotion. The one thing that seems certain is that Ms. Kardashian has all the self-esteem she needs. She loves herself.

Ms. Kardashian has several occupations. She's a fashion designer, a video producer, an author, and a model. But the main activity fueling all of her far-flung projects is that of simply being a celebrity. She knows how to get media attention. No one attracts publicity like Kim does. It's as if she were born to it. Perhaps she was.

She arrived in the right place, and had the right parents. If your life's work is exploitation of the publicity machine, there's nowhere better to start than Beverly Hills. Kim was born there in 1980. Her dad, Robert Kardashian, was a prominent California lawyer. He gained fame in 1994 with his work as chief counsel for O.J. Simpson's defense team. Kim's mom, Kris, had been best friends with murder victim Nicole Simpson. The O.J. trial made celebrities out of just about anyone it touched. The Kardashians didn't mind. They knew the value of publicity.

Kim's first media exposure came from her friendship with another celebrity's celebrity, Paris Hilton. When Ms. Hilton began attracting tabloid coverage, Kim climbed aboard for the ride. She had a high-profile divorce from her first husband, music producer Damon Thomas, then a short, but tumultuous relationship with singer Ray J. Her image was all over the media, but she was almost always playing a supporting role for Ms. Hilton.

In 2007 two events occurred that changed everything. The first was the leak of a compromising video of Kim with Ray J. It was a "private" tape the couple had recorded four years earlier. The recording went viral, creating the kind of sensationalism that could ruin a young woman's career. Instead, Kim treated it as an opportunity. Her initial move was guaranteed to increase her publicity. She sued the company responsible for the video, and settled for a payment in the millions. Then, later that year, she and the rest of her family agreed to have their lives chronicled in a new reality TV series.

Robert Kardashian had died in 2003, but he and Kim's mother, Kris, had already been divorced for years. Not long after the divorce, Kris Kardashian had remarried, this time to Olympic star Bruce Jenner. This couple, along with Kim and two of her sisters, were the main stars of the reality show: Keeping Up With the

Kardashians. It became one of the biggest hits of the decade.

Since then Kim has become the most famous Kardashian, as well as their biggest moneymaker. Her fame and fortune are based entirely on style. She recognizes the need for total self- absorption if she's going to reach her goals. When the cameras roll, she knows how to make herself the center of every picture. Kim finds her own activities are fascinating. She invites us to be fascinated, too. Enough of us go along to keep her ratings high and her fashion lines selling.

So far this has resulted in a net worth of over $20 million. The longer we remain fascinated with her, the larger her fortune will grow.

What does Ms. Kardashian have that others don't? That's easy: confidence, self-esteem, and a complete sense of who she is and what she wants. Kim Kardashian loves herself, and what might be even more important, she likes herself. She's comfortable with who she is.

She knows what every successful job seeker and every good entrepreneur must know: how to use this confidence to get where she wants to go.

Her main product is her image. Kim's image gets the ratings, sells the fashion and fragrance lines, and fuels every Kardashian endeavor. That image depends on her. Take Kim out of the equation, and the image disappears. Without her presence there are no TV appearances, or books, or clothes, or even the hint of a fragrance. Though a lot depends on her, she doesn't acknowledge any pressure. She knows she can handle it. This kind of confidence is necessary in any business, even those whose products aren't as personal as hers.

Serena

Serena started her business with a novel idea: wake-up calls complete with power breakfasts for visiting businesspeople staying in local motels. Living in a resort city that caters to meetings and conventions, Serena has spent most of her working life in jobs that serve traveling businesspeople. She's waited tables, tended bar, clerked at hotel and motel desks, and she ran one hotel's room service operations. Many motel tenants have told her what they'd like most is a real meal in the morning, but they're often too rushed and disorganized to do more than grab a stale muffin from the motel's paltry "complimentary breakfast" area.

Serena imagined a way to change that. What if someone staying in a local motel for a few days of meetings could arrange for a combination of wake-up calls and in-room breakfasts for each day of his or her visit? This customer could preselect from a short menu with a few different basic styles of breakfast. These would include options ranging from light continental to health food to traditional bacon & eggs. The customer could pick a basic motif, and let the chef choose the details, or order a la carte by midnight the night before. At the prearranged time the meal would arrive at the door, along with a wake-up phone call.

Serena had the contacts to get her service into several motels. She had a site for her kitchen, and the beginnings of a good staff. But her idea was novel. She couldn't point to independent market research because there hadn't been any. She knew of no other businesses that provided this. What Serena needed was a ton of self-confidence. She needed to sell herself to potential investors.

A local banker names Mr. Sayles arranged for Serena to meet with a prospective investor. This was Ms. Betty Freed, a retired Realtor who wanted to back the efforts of local women. Ms. Freed had read Serena's business proposal, and was intrigued. She thought the idea might work.

They met in the banker's office. After they shook hands, Ms. Freed sat down and said: "Okay, Serena, wow me. You can start by telling me why you want to start this business."

Serena heard the question and her mind froze. "Well . . ." she started, then she let silence fill the room.

Her mind worked furiously, yet she had no clear thoughts. "Uh . . . I thought I explained that in the proposal."

"Did you? Maybe you did. But tell me what you're thinking right this minute. What makes you want to do this?"

"Uh . . . I don't think it's ever been tried. It's new. I think it could be exciting, don't you?"

Ms. Freed stared at her. "I suppose it could, but I'm having a hard time envisioning it."

"But didn't you read the proposal?" Serena asked.

"Of course I did, but let's pretend I didn't. Let's say I know nothing about your business, so you have to explain it from scratch. The best place to start is your reason for wanting to do it."

"I think there's a market. I laid all that out in there." She pointed to a copy of the proposal on the banker's desk. "The motels on Route 8 average two thousand business visitors a week, each staying an average of three days. That's a potential of six thousand breakfasts. If we could get just 5% of them . . ."

Ms. Freed smiled and interrupted. "Serena, I read the facts and figures. You make them persuasive on paper. Make them come alive for me here and now."

"B-But don't the numbers speak for themselves?" Serena asked.

"No," said Ms. Freed. "They never do. Let's forget my question. I'm guessing you have a presentation for me."

"Uh, yes." As Serena stumbled haltingly through a ner-vous recitation of numbers and logic, along with a PowerPoint show, Ms. Freed listened. When Serena wasn't yet halfway done, the older woman held up her hand. "Stop, Serena."

"Of course," said Serena. "What do you need to know?"

"I have an observation," Ms. Freed started. "You have an interesting, untested idea. You've never tried to woo an investor before, so you're counting on your idea to persuade me. I like the idea, but, like any smart investor, I'm not thrilled by the fact that no one's done it before. It doesn't give me much to go on. The one thing I do have is you. Your proposal is fine. The problem is with your presentation of you, yourself. That's what you're selling. I wouldn't be here if I didn't already like your idea. I'm sure you can put together a competent staff. I know you have a pool of potential customers. But you must convince me you can inspire your staff, fascinate your customers, and deliver a quality product. That means you should know exactly why you want to start this business. It means you should be able to help me picture your business, and how it would look to the customer opening her motel room door first thing in the morning. You have to inspire me, and you aren't going to do it with numbers or dry logic. You're going to do it with you. I need to know that this is truly your dream, and that you can sell that dream."

"But I can," Serena protested.

"I believe you," said Ms. Freed. "That's why I want to give you another chance. Let's meet again in two days. In the meantime, think about how this business connects with your heart and soul."

"Uh . . . okay."

"I'll be ready to start fresh and hear you out," Ms. Freed promised.

"Yes," Serena said hesitantly. "Fresh."

Ms. Freed exited, leaving Serena alone with Mr. Sayles.

"Looks like you have your work cut out for you," he said.

"What do I do?" Serena pleaded.

"Exactly what she suggested," said Sayles. "Sell yourself to her."

Serena went through the rest of the day in something close to shock. Her imagination abandoned her. She read her own proposal, and lost faith. By the time she went to bed she was convinced that her idea was doomed.

Then, in the morning she woke up, looked at the ceiling, then closed her eyes. "I'm in a motel room," she told herself. "I have meetings all day. I'll be listening, talking, and making choices. What do I need to find in three minutes, when I open my motel room door?"

In her mind she began to smell the coffee.

The following morning Serena arrived at Mr. Sayles' office early. When Ms. Freed entered, a brightly colored box sat on the table. Inside was Ms. Freed's breakfast. The croissant was perfect, as was the three-minute egg. The cinnamon toast was Ms. Freed's favorite. The juice was fresh-squeezed. Serena had done her homework on Ms. Freed's breakfast habits.

"It's designed for great taste, high energy, and all-morning stamina," said Serena. "In other words, I designed it for you. It's one of the key features of my service. I know how I want my breakfast. My job is to learn how you want yours, if possible without asking you. A quick internet search can often provide clues for the extra touches. A call to your secretary helped, too."

"Did she suggest the copy of the *Wall Street Journal*?" Ms. Freed asked.

"I read your business profile in an online e-zine," said Serena. "You said you prefer a hard copy to the one on your Kindle. You want to know what I'm all about. I'm all about you, the customer. My entire goal is to make the first meal of your day a success, including the newspaper. If I do that, you've got a much better chance to succeed in whatever you do."

Ms. Freed smiled. "Not bad." Then she took a bite of her croissant.

With her self-confidence restored, Serena got Ms. Freed's backing. Within a few months her business was thriving. Serena calls herself "Queen of the Wake-Up Call," and she appears in all of her online promotions. She's usually featured cooking breakfast. She likes to gaze into the camera lens and say: "I'm all about breaking eggs—the first step in creating your perfect omelet!" She's working on the "Wake-Up Call Cookbook." It will have plenty of recipes, but its most essential ingredient will be Serena, herself.

WRESTLING WITH DESTINY

In previous chapters we've looked at some famous people and how they achieved success. If there's one thread uniting almost all of their stories, it's that getting there is half the fun. That doesn't mean it's easy, or even that it's fun all the time, but most successful people recall their struggles for success fondly. They loved the challenges, and the sense that even their setbacks (perhaps the setbacks most of all) were opportunities to learn and grow. Success seldom happens overnight. It takes preparation, nurturing, and long months of persistence and patience. So you shouldn't be in too much of a hurry. Hurrying leads to carelessness, and carelessness can sink a business before it opens its doors.

John and Jane Doe

In many of these examples we've seen the importance of preparation. It's almost always a key ingredient in success stories. John Doe and Jane Doe might have similar ideas for starting their ventures, but if Jane does her homework, and John doesn't do his, which one is more likely to succeed? Both are starting restaurants. John envisions his floor plan, talks with cooks, creates his menu, and thinks about how big his kitchen needs to be. He's looked at websites and catalogues, but he hasn't paid much attention to prices. John hasn't even made an estimate of his operating budget when suddenly he finds a site. It seems to be a good location at a bargain price, so he signs a lease right away. The lease doesn't start for a month, and he uses the time to imagine what he'll do when he gets in there. But he feels like finding the place is such an achievement that he deserves a break. He decides to take a few days off at the ocean just to recharge his engines. He doesn't consider the fact that he's paying with an almost maxed-out credit card.

When Jane starts imagining her restaurant, she begins her research immediately. As things occur to her, she asks questions, makes calls, and looks things up. She talks to bankers and potential investors, asking specific questions and receiving tentative commitments. She checks out licensing and zoning requirements, calculates overhead, payroll, and taxes, and looks for just the right site. She doesn't jump at anything, allowing herself to learn from the process. Once she finds a location, she knows what she has to work with, and she begins to adapt her planning to what she actually has. She returns to her finance people, and turns their commitments into actual funds. Within a week she brings in a crew to remodel the kitchen. Within six weeks she has all her inspections, permits, and licenses in place. While John is still looking up suppliers' addresses and struggling with bureaucratic forms, Jane is putting the final touches on decorations for her Grand Opening.

When Jane has opened her doors, and she's got the neighborhood buzzing about her business, her real work has just begun. She learns that running a business means having an endless string of decisions. As she sorts through these, questions emerge. The business is up and running, but where is it going to go? If this restaurant succeeds, might she want to open a second one? Can her business plan for one restaurant evolve into a plan for a chain? Or might Jane decide to specialize in baked goods? Should she sell these goods wholesale to other restaurants? Farther down the road, her incredibly varied menu might draw enough attention that her customers urge her to write a cookbook. When the book becomes a monster success, Jane sells her restaurant interests, and concentrates on being a best-selling food writer. She adapts to her evolving destiny.

Every entrepreneur has a destiny, but when the first business opens it's not always clear what that destiny is. At the dawn of Apple, Steve Jobs saw his future in desktop computing, but his path led through other new companies and new media, including animation, filmmaking, and finally back to Apple. There he steered his old company into the brave new world of mobile devices. Similarly, Oprah began as a local newscaster. At the start her only goal was having her own syndicated show. Ten years later she was well on her way to building an empire that would eventually include a magazine, books, and TV and film productions. Both of them had destinies that weren't clear at the start. Both took advantage of every opportunity to shape those destinies.

We tend to think of the future success story as being someone who's always in a hurry. While it's true that the best entrepreneurs act quickly, they also wait for the right moment. They know that patience is essential as one's destiny unfolds. In an earlier chapter we saw how rapper Jay Z struggled through the early part of his career, often giving in to violent urges, and following his worst instincts. When he finally began to exercise patience, his moments came, one after the other. In a little over a decade he built one of the largest fortunes in the music business.

At Kentucky Fried Chicken, Sam Su found himself shaping the destiny of an international company's China division. He searched for a way to adapt a hugely successful business model to what now promises to become the world's biggest market. He had to remake KFC into a Chinese enterprise, yet it still had to be KFC. He looked at the essence of each—the company and the country—and found the points where they could connect. A quarter-century later his effort is a textbook example of how to adapt a model to a new market.

Whatever her path, Jane will be well-prepared. This readiness allows her to employ patience. She knows that most worthwhile efforts take time to reach fulfillment. When an opportunity presents itself, Jane is always there, ready to take advantage of it. At such a moment she might appear to move with lightning speed. In fact, Jane has already done the important work. Her preparations allow her to act without hesitation, adapting to conditions that change every day. She's always ready to exploit opportunities to improve, or try something new, but she always waits for the proper moments, when preparations and opportunities combine to give her the best chance for success. She knows that patience, persistence, flexibility, and hard work are guideposts on the path to a happy destiny.

CHAPTER ELEVEN: THE POWER OF POSITIVE THINKING: HOW TO APPLY WHAT WE'VE LEARNED

Negativity breeds more negativity, but positive thinking yields positive results. Every successful entrepreneur knows this. Sixty-one years ago Norman Vincent Peale wrote one of the biggest bestsellers in history: *The Power of Positive Thinking*. More recently, Australian TV writer Rhonda Byrne had similar success with her book and DVD, both titled: *The Secret*. She starts with a basic principle that should be obvious to all of us: If you always believe that you can reach your goal, you're virtually certain to get there.

Byrne and Peale both use variations of an exercise in which you envision what you want in order to make it happen. This starts with imagining your goal. The better you can see it, the better your chance of reaching it. Oprah imagined herself as stepping onto the same stage with presidents, kings, and queens. After years of progressing one small step at a time, she made it happen. Kim Kardashian wanted all the trappings of success, using herself and her life as her own main products. As a model she owned the runway. Starting as a support character in reality TV, she quickly emerged as the star. Viewers were fascinated by her unashamed self-promotion. She made self-absorption into her signature, and played her self-created role to the hilt. Her efforts have made her millions.

There are clear lessons here. Always concentrate on solutions rather than problems. Always look at what you need to succeed, and root out those things that imply failure.

Your "EQ"

Healthy emotions are just as important as a healthy intellect. You must keep a healthy EQ to go with your IQ. We all know what "IQ" is—a number indicating an individual's basic intelligence. IQ tests are designed to measure the power of our intellects. How well can we follow logical sequences? How well can we identify particular things and actions? Can we recognize, analyze, and draw correct conclusions? Those are the basics of an intelligent quotient, or "IQ." "EQ" is shorthand for emotional intelligence quotient. It's a measurement of one's ability to perceive, control, analyze, and evaluate emotions. Most entrepreneurs will find that this ability is every bit as important as intellectual prowess. They know the value of trusting their gut reactions.

A lot of what goes into EQ is simple maturity. If you have control of your emotions, that always gives you an edge. Successes won't blind you, and failures won't send you spiraling into depression. When you're emotionally mature you can take life as it comes, accepting what's there so that you can shape it to your needs. This doesn't mean you always have to be cool and calm. A mature person might feel elation, sorrow, courage, fear, or any other emotion. These feelings might be as strong or stronger than anyone else's. The difference is in approach. The person with a good EQ will be able to handle it. Someone with emotional maturity will channel strong feelings into productive action. An immature person will give in to the emotion, allowing it to rule his or her actions.

When Jay Z learned to channel his anger, transforming it into intelligent action, the result was huge success and incredible wealth. After escaping an early life filled with abuse and trauma, Oprah used her negative feelings to produce positive energy. That energy built one of the world's largest, most influential business empires. Floyd Mayweather emerged from his troubled childhood with an ability to train and fight. He could've taken this fighting ability out on the street, or into his home, and lived a criminal life of violence. Instead he chose the boxing ring, where he could turn his violent urges into a sports success story.

Your Success Story

Are you ready for your success story? Are you willing to take a good long look at yourself, accepting the reality of whatever you see, while identifying things that need improvement? Can you learn patience? Can you adapt to change? Perhaps the most important fundamental skill in all this is having a positive attitude. This begins with your feelings about yourself. As you examine your intellect, emotions, and overall temperament, do you feel good about yourself? Do you like the person in the mirror? Are you comfortable with who and what you are?

Can you identify your weaknesses? If so, can you correct them, overcome them, or compensate for them?

Can you accept your imperfections without guilt? Can you find their causes? Make changes? Can you overcome your flaws, and learn from new experiences?

Positive thinking always involves challenges. It's a way to meet those challenges, understand them, and create solutions. Positive thinking is the process of success. Everything else we've covered here depends on it. Preparation, adaptation, self- confidence, lifelong learning, and taking responsibility all sit on a foundation of positive thinking. Long-term success is impossible without it.

You are all CEOs. Even first-time job seekers are the chief executive officers of their own lives. We all make dozens of decisions every day. Each day we decide, consciously or unconsciously, what our lives will be like. Some of us choose slow decline, while others decide to tread water. But there are those of us who make the choice to be the best that we can be. We look at the world, and see ways we might improve it. We identify what people need, and find methods to provide them with it. That's the road to success. If it's real success, it will bring you happiness. That's the real goal in all of this.

Remember: an unhappy billionaire is no better off than an unhappy ditch digger. So be sure you begin by doing something you care about enough that you want to do it well, then give it all you've got. That's what jobs, businesses, and any worthwhile efforts are all about.

ABOUT THE AUTHOR

Malcolm Allen is a recognized expert on human potential and (BCSA) Board Certified Social Advocate. He migrates effortlessly between corporate boardrooms and underserved communities aiming to advance the interests of social justice, particularly on behalf of populations or groups who have been disadvantaged, disempowered, or forgotten.

Allen has authored over two dozen books, and most have achieved best-selling status. He has worked with subject matter experts and credentialed instruction designers to socially engineer a platform of outcome-based programs that provide solutions for disabled veterans, recidivism, human trafficking, dropout prevention, bullying, diversity, mentoring, financial inclusion, entrepreneurship, and leadership. All programs are Military Approved, and available at

Penn Foster College and Graduate America Centers of Excellence around the world. For seminar licensing, book purchases, or speaker requests, please visit: Unconditional.org